MW00489982

SHUT UP AND WRITE THE BOOK

A STEP-BY-STEP GUIDE TO CRAFTING YOUR NOVEL FROM PLAN TO PRINT

JENNA MORECI

SHUT UP AND WRITE THE BOOK:
A Step-by-Step Guide to Crafting Your Novel From Plan to Print

For inquiries, please direct all mailed correspondence to:
PO Box 475
San Carlos, CA 94070
USA

ISBN: 978-0-9997352-7-5 (hardback)
ISBN: 978-0-9997352-8-2 (paperback)
ISBN: 978-0-9997352-9-9 (ebook)

www.JennaMoreci.com
Edited by Bound by Words and Kimberly Cannon
Book Cover by Miblart
Graphics by Grace Treadaway

SHUT UP AND AND WRITE THE BOOK

A STEP-BY-STEP GUIDE
TO CRAFTING YOUR NOVEL
FROM PLAN TO PRINT

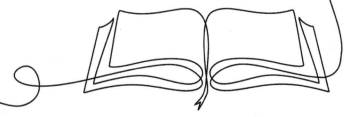

JENNA MORECI

CONTENTS

SHUT UP AND READ THIS FIRST

Writing a book is hard.

You probably already know that. I imagine you've picked up this guide for that very reason. Either you're deep in the throes of writerly chaos, or you're just getting started and already overwhelmed.

I've been there. My passion for writing began in the first grade, and I've started countless manuscripts since then, only to toss my hands up in defeat fifty or so pages in. Thus, I spent over twenty years researching the art of storytelling, honing my craft, and perfecting my method. It was only through this steadfast investigation (okay, obsession) that I was finally able to finish a novel—which turned into multiple novels, which turned into Amazon and Audible bestsellers and award winners. I'm now living what I'd heard was an impossible dream: the life of a career author. But I couldn't have gotten to this place without all those late hours, painstaking revisions, and slow spirals into creative madness.

That's in large part why I started my YouTube channel, *Writing with Jenna Moreci*. I know firsthand how daunting a writer's journey can be, especially when you're on your own. I didn't have any mentors or guidance. There certainly weren't any writing channels I could watch online, mostly because YouTube didn't exist yet, but let's sidestep my ancient origins for the time being. The point is, I was alone on this journey for well over a decade, and that's what made it so awful.

I don't want you to go through that.

Which brings us to this book. After years of trial and error, I've developed a step-by-step formula for crafting a novel from conception to completion. The idea phase, outlining, drafting, editing—this system covers it all in specific detail, leaving the wiggle room needed to spread your wings where you see fit. There's a sense of comfort that comes with knowing each step of the infinite ladder of drafting. It's a north star to guide you, simplifying the journey into a methodical routine.

Now I'm sharing that routine with you.

Writing will always be hard. I can't promise you restful nights, perfect first drafts, or bestselling novels. But I can provide an action plan that will make the process a whole lot less overwhelming. My goal is to give you the proper steps to reach the finish line—to set you up as best as I can for success.

Want to actually *finish* your manuscript? That's what I'm here for.

Is this book for you?

If you're a fiction writer who is new to the gig, intimidated by the task, or simply looking to refine your process, keep reading. Novices and established authors alike could learn a thing or twelve. If I'm still growing in my creativity, you should be too.

Do you want a step-by-step guide to writing a novel? Do you want each stage mapped out in (mostly) sequential order with detailed definitions and tips? Do you want to know the "why" behind writerly practices alongside thorough breakdowns of techniques so you can choose what's best suited for your story and skill level? Then this book is for you.

If you're writing any form of nonfiction, from self-help to memoirs, I'm afraid you're in the wrong place. This guide covers all facets of fiction from selecting a genre to structuring a plot and crafting characters. We're here to study the art of imaginary people and places, not to dabble in the real world.

If you're looking for marketing and publishing advice, the bad news continues. This book is all about *writing*: outlining, drafting, editing, and all things that bring pen to page or fingers to keyboard. If I delved into the ins and outs of publishing, we'd be looking at a dictionary-length tome—a weapon, really. How about we save that for another book? Instead, this guide tackles how to efficiently and effectively complete a manuscript—one you can print out and gently rock in your arms like the precious book baby it is.

Or cackle over it maniacally. It's your baby. Do you.

What can you expect?

I'm a proponent of straightforward, no bullshit advice. I mean, this book has "shut up" in the title. Delicacy left the station a long time ago. Blame the fact that I'm all out of fucks to give, but I believe the best way to explain something is the simplest way. This book isn't going to beat around the bush, and if some salty language makes you blush, maybe seek education elsewhere.

If you want all your decisions validated, I'm not your woman. Sure, writing without a plan works for some authors, but not for many. No, you can't release a quality novel without an editor. I wrote this book to help you create the best story you can, and that means providing honest truths based off years of experience (and mistakes). Of course, you're entitled to make your own choices. Some of my tips might not work for you or may need modifying to fit your writing style. Hell, you might decide to ignore my advice entirely. That's your call. But my job, as your handy-dandy guide, is to prepare you as best I can for this monumental undertaking, and that means telling it like it is.

Looking for other books, apps, and software to help you as you write? I've scattered various tools throughout these chapters and listed them in the resource guide in the back of the book. Please note, I have affiliate arrangements with a few of these platforms, which means I receive a small commission if you choose to make a purchase through the applicable link. This does not affect the price of the product, nor does it affect my opinion. Your trust matters to me, and I wouldn't risk my reputation for a buck here or there. If you see a resource mentioned, it's because I've found it beneficial to my career, and it might benefit you too.

Still with me? Wonderful. You might be nervous sweating already, in which case I'm glad I can't smell you. Grab a glass of water and take some deep breaths. Writing a book doesn't have to be as hard as it seems, or as hard as it's been thus far. Allow this guide to organize your muddled thoughts and keep you headed in the right direction. There will be bumps in the road and plenty of aggravation, but you'll also experience immense pride and moments of brilliance. You're on the path of writing *your very own book*. Even better, you're not doing this alone.

Now shut up and get to reading.

CHAPTER 1
WHAT THE HELL SHOULD I WRITE ABOUT?

CHOOSING A TOPIC AIN'T ALWAYS EASY

BEFORE YOU PUT a single word on the page, you need to have a workable idea. This may sound obvious, but plenty of people dive headfirst into the writing process without having a firm grasp of the story they're trying to tell. Pump the breaks, take a seat, and prepare for some serious soul-searching. I know, it seems like a boring first step when all you want to do is write, but I promise it will be worth it. Sure, you can open a document and start typing, but eventually the words—and your motivation—will fizzle out. Doing some brainstorming up front will expedite the writing and completing of your manuscript, which is the whole reason you're reading this book, right?

You may already know exactly what you want to write. If that's the case, feel free to scoot on over to the next chapter. But if your imagination has run dry, or you've got notebooks full of ideas but aren't sure where to begin, these handy tips will help you generate topics fueled by passion, then whittle them away until only one remains: the premise for your wondrous, magical book baby.

Let's start with the hard part, shall we?

COME UP WITH IDEAS...OBVIOUSLY

When people ask how writers scrounge up ideas, you often hear the same responses:

"Read more."

"Watch TV."

But it's far more nuanced than that. The number one tool for being a creator is to have a *truly creative mind*. Many aspiring authors claim they want to write a book, but they also don't consider themselves creative. Even when they read stacks of fiction or seek out inspiration, their brain feels constipated, unwilling to drum up anything fresh or unique.

Drawing a blank in the idea department can be extremely frustrating. You may want to quit before you've even started. Fortunately, there's a well-kept secret to becoming an idea-generating cyborg:

All you have to do is think shit up.

But Jenna, that's my problem. I can't think of anything!

Sure you can. After all, how do you pick the clothes you wear each day? How do you choose the words that come out of your mouth? How do you select which restaurant you want takeout from? It's all basic thought and decision-making. Coming up with story ideas is the same thing.

Have you ever thought up what-if scenarios on your commute to work, or while overhearing an argument between two strangers in a coffee shop? People create fiction every day without even realizing it. Do you remember creating worlds, storylines, and imaginary friends as a child? When I was in Kindergarten, I regularly pretended to be a baby boy cobra named Boobie. Do you have an equally embarrassing story? You better. I can't be the only one oversharing among us.

You've made something out of nothing countless times before. There's no reason you can't apply this same practice to your writing. You've got a big, beautiful brain at your disposal. Use it.

Sometimes cooking up ideas requires a jump start, and that's when outside influences come into play. Creativity begets creativity, so if you're looking to spark your imagination, surround yourself with creative energy through whatever means suit you best.

If you're a visual person, create physical or digital representations that speak to you, or discover art that gets your wheels turning. Make collages of face claims for your characters, collect images that reflect your story's aesthetic, or piece together mood boards that emulate the themes you want your writing to convey. If you're an artist, immerse yourself in the medium that most inspires you.

If music is your go-to inspiration source, writing playlists are a game changer. I have playlists devoted to individual characters, themes, and novels, where each song mirrors a particular chapter or scene within the story. Sometimes I listen to music while I write, but often I listen while I'm running errands, doing chores, showering, or winding down to sleep. All the while, storylines are playing in my mind, and suddenly I have an endless stream of ideas without having touched my keyboard.

If the written word inspires you, devour books or poetry in genres you love. If you're more of a cinema buff, watch your favorite films and pay close attention to how they make you feel. How can your story generate the same reactions in your future readers?

If you're inspired by the world around you, explore. Travel to new places that stimulate your mind, or simply spend an afternoon in your backyard. Go on a hike, take a walk, get moving, and get creating.

Figure out what works for you and put your imagination to work. If it helps, set a reminder on your phone, or make a date with yourself to be creative at least once a week. The more dedicated you are to this process, the longer your list of potential story concepts will be.

CHILL OUT

If you're still overwhelmed, let's chat about relaxation. At this point in time, the thought of writing shouldn't stress you out, so we need to smooth out those wrinkles before tackling your book.

Why have you decided to embark on this journey in the first place? I'd wager it wasn't for the money or the fame; if that's your motivation, you're either not very attuned to the writing industry, or you've got worms in your brain. I imagine you're here because you *love to write*. It's a creative endeavor that puts your imagination first. You're at the helm of a unique and phenomenal story that you've concocted, beautifully tailored to your personal tastes and desires.

You experience enough pressure on the daily. Writing should be an escape, not a burden.

Make it fun

Children are inherently and wildly creative. Have you ever watched a child play with a cardboard box? To them, it becomes a rocket ship, a magical cave, or a palace. That's the crux of imagination: It's play. Somewhere down the line you may have lost that part of you, possibly because of your parents, school, or society as a whole sucking the joy out of your tender artist's heart. It's time to take the fun back. If you think about it, you're inventing characters, conflicts, and worlds with your imagination. That is the definition of playtime.

You've been stifling your inner child for far too long, and the poor thing is probably bored to tears. Let them live a little. You'll both appreciate it.

Unwind

Many writers worry about cover art, publication dates, and above all else, reader opinion before they've even written a word. The tension builds, feeding on any semblance of creativity.

Not only is this intense stress unnecessary, but it also prevents the writing process from being any fun—which, as we already covered, is kind of important.

Have you ever had a story idea when you were about to fall asleep, or while taking a shower? We writers get our best ideas when we're relaxed, so this is an important trick to master. Easing open that pressure valve will do your imagination a world of good.

No judgments allowed

Another reason children are so much more creative than adults is because they don't embarrass as easily. They haven't yet experienced the shame that comes with age, which means they typically feel free to make mistakes. That's a mindset you'll need to relearn if you want to be a more creative writer. Give yourself the green light to come up with as many ideas as you want, no matter how ridiculous or self-indulgent.

No, seriously. *Any* idea. I don't care if it's completely bonkers. Jot it down.

Remember, just because you have an idea doesn't mean you have to write about it. Embracing the freedom to produce anything you desire means abandoning all limitations on your imagination. In turn, you'll generate more ideas at a rapid pace, and you'll have more content to work with.

But Jenna, won't some of these ideas suck?

Not some of them—most of them. Sometimes your imagination is a mind-vagina birthing spectacular wisdom, and other times it's a mind-anus spewing shit. But when you put a cap on your creativity, you're stifling all areas of invention. Sure, the garbage won't surface, but neither will the brilliance.

Allow yourself to be an idiot, and I promise you'll find some genius in it. The worst thing that can happen is your story turns out to be no good, in which case, you can delete it and try again. This is your space to explore the wonderful ideas in your head. No one is watching, and this time is for you and you alone to express your artistry.

EXAMINE THE MARKET

This is a vital step that's often mishandled by aspiring authors. Many writers skip this step entirely, or they put far too much weight on it, stifling their own creativity in the process.

I get it. This book is your art. It's your passion. But you're also planning to exchange it with customers for cash, which means it's a product to be sold. Congratulations, you're officially a businessperson, and it behooves you to study the industry you're entering.

What are the current trends within the writing and publishing business? Which genres are on the outs? Which categories are making a comeback? Which niches are thriving? Understanding the market means understanding your place within it, and that will make both the writing and marketing process a whole lot easier to navigate. Eventually, you'll want to examine the industry further, analyzing advertising strategies, author platform best practices, and cover art trends, but don't worry about that yet. Right now, your focus is singular: Which books are people reading, and why?

But Jenna, I've already done this step!

You might have overdone this step, in fact. That's where the second oopsie comes into play—you've strategized to your own detriment. Don't be the person who selects a story concept because a successful author already wrote it, or solely because it's trendy.

It's true when people say everything's been done before. There will always be books about demons, magic, true love, and betrayal. It's perfectly fine to write about any of these topics; I've covered the latter three myself. But there's a difference between utilizing common tropes and using a popular novel as a blueprint for your work in progress.

Just because you love a book series doesn't mean you should copy and paste those exact concepts into your manuscript. Relying on another author to generate ideas for you means abandoning what it takes to be a creative writer. In fact, it isn't considered creating at all. It's valid to find inspiration in stories you admire, but add your own unique take on plot dynamics, subplots, characters, and relationships. This breathes originality into a concept, and that's what readers are hungry for.

After creating your own ideas, trust your instincts and imagination. It's okay if your book features a dystopian society, but if your heroine is an impoverished teen archer who volunteers to compete in a deadly competition, it might be time to rethink your direction.

Along with not regurgitating your favorite stories, it's best to avoid trend-chasing just for the sake of it. This may go against some advice given within the writing community. For what it's worth, there's absolutely nothing wrong with writing an on-trend book; in fact, it works in your favor. But choosing a story concept for the sole purpose of fitting into a trend is another beast entirely, and it's one you should probably steer clear of.

For starters, it takes a long time to write a book, especially if it's your first. That means by the time your book comes out, this trend might be long gone. And if you're writing a series, forget it. What happens when you release book one and the trend is already outdated?

Second, if you hop on a trend strictly for readership, you're probably not going to be all that invested in your story. Passion oozes off the pages of a novel, and it's even more apparent if the passion is nonexistent. Your story likely won't have that oomph readers crave, and even worse, you'll probably have a terrible time writing it. How can you rationalize spending years toiling over a project with no guarantee of success when you don't even enjoy the process? Remember, writing is supposed to be fun.

If you're passionate about a concept that happens to be on trend, by all means, have at it. Either way, your joy or lack thereof will show in your writing.

WRITE WHAT YOU WANT TO READ

I'd argue this is the most important step in this part of the writing process. A lot of people will tell you that when it comes to fiction, you should write what you want to write. But there's a better suggestion out there, and Robin McKinley said it best: Write what you want to *read*. Often what you want to write and what you want to read overlap, but there can be a few discrepancies.

I love writing dialogue, especially banter. But if I were to solely write what I wanted to write, I'd have a book filled with snarky jokes, playful flirtations, and little else. As much as I enjoy a giggle fit, endless sarcasm does not a story make.

Put your go-to writing aside and ask yourself, what story have you been looking for but haven't been able to find yet?

"If there's a book that you want to read, but it hasn't been written yet, then you must write it." – Toni Morrison

Listen, Morrison knew what she was talking about.

There are many reasons it's a great idea to write what you want to read. If it's a concept you'd read, that means your heart is involved. You'll be invested in the storyline because it contains elements that excite you. It's a lot easier to ride out the difficult parts of the writing process when you deeply care about the material and genuinely believe in its message.

Let's not forget the fact that, if you want to read the story, chances are other people will want to read it too. Some folks feel like their tastes are too unique, but there's a niche for everything. Hell, dinosaur erotica has a vibrant, thriving audience. I promise your story isn't nearly as obscure as you think.

Be honest with yourself. What story calls to you? What would you like to see more of in fiction? Which idea keeps coming back into your mind throughout the day? If you're going to spend countless hours and grueling effort writing a story to completion, it should be one you feel deeply connected to. This is about gut instinct. Which idea speaks to you louder than all the rest?

Sometimes it's not the most obvious choice. Before writing my dark fantasy romance novel, *The Savior's Champion*, I had a different concept already outlined in full—a Cinderella retelling with a fleshed out cast of characters and a vibrant world. But something about it didn't feel right. I craved darker, more dangerous content, along with a much deeper, mature love story. *The Savior's Champion* was the concept that provided this for me, and truthfully, it was the exact kind of story I was dying to read at the time. I didn't have an outline—hell, I didn't even know my main character's name—but it didn't matter. I chose the concept I couldn't get out of my head, and it was one of the smartest business decisions I've ever made.

Take on the task of creating those characters, those conflicts, and that world. The passion and commitment you bleed onto the pages will attract readers who share the same excitement as you.

PASSION AND MARKETING CAN (AND SHOULD) COEXIST

At this point, you should have a list of potential ideas. You're relaxed, you've examined the market, and you've found the type of fiction that gets your juices flowing. But what happens when two or more ideas are at the finish line, waiting for you to break the tie?

This can be a big stopping-point for a lot of writers. You've already consulted your gut when it comes to these ideas, and you're invested in finishing this novel. Now it's time to turn on the practical side of your brain and consult your industry research. Remember, you're an artist *and* a businessperson now. Consider this your first business decision.

Which idea is performing best in the current market?

Trend-chasing for the sake of it isn't ideal, but if readers are ravenous for a genre that happens to encapsulate one of your favorite ideas, then that's an opportunity worth snatching up. If another idea fits into a genre that's currently on the outs, it's probably wise to keep it on the backburner for now.

Which idea would be quicker or easier to write?

All writers want to start their book as quickly as possible, but finishing that book is its own struggle. If completion is a recurring issue for you, identify if one of your ideas is shorter or simpler than the others. If there is one, it should be a definite contender for your attention. Getting a few finished pieces under your belt is great motivation for completing harder projects in the future.

Which idea would suit you best at this stage of your writing journey?

Say you're a mere babe of a writer, and you have two ideas for your next work in progress. One is an epic fantasy spanning hundreds of worlds and generations, and the other is the introspective journey of a single character you connect with on a deep level. Which story would you feel most confident tackling first? As writers, we build our craft the more we write. Taking the time to learn and grow can be a huge asset before tackling more complex projects.

FROM IDEA TO PREMISE

Congratulations, you've chosen an idea! But if you're anything like the writers I know, your idea may be some vague mishmash of words that only sort of fit together.

When I first came up with my idea for *The Savior's Champion*, it sounded something like this:

An underground gladiatorial tournament. Twenty dudes compete in deadly challenges. Winner gets a bride. There are killer statues, hanging vines, a dark tunnel, a falling floor, and ominous red paint.

Um . . . What?

Sure, all these concepts made their way into my story, but none of them equate to a *premise*. Most, if not all, pieces of fiction revolve around a **conflict** the main character must overcome or a **goal** they're fighting to achieve. That, right there, is your premise: the plot of your novel told in its simplest terms.

How can you rework your idea into a conflict or goal?

The conflict of *The Savior's Champion* is two-part: My main character, Tobias, is fighting to stay alive in a deadly tournament. He's also fallen for a woman he's not supposed to be with. His goal, however, is singular: escape the tournament with the woman he loves.

Just like that, my nonsensical idea has turned into the premise for a novel—something I can build on.

At this point, you should know what type of story you're aiming to write next—at least in general terms. Even though we're going to begin planning your novel in the next chapter, I want you to hold on to the concepts from this one. They're the necessary foundation for building the life of your book.

SUMMARY

WHAT THE HELL SHOULD I WRITE ABOUT?

- Keenly observe the world around you and take notes. Coming up with ideas is as simple as creating what-if scenarios.

- Consume art and partake in activities that inspire your creativity.

- Chill out. The more you relax, the more creative ideas will naturally come to you.

- Know that some of your ideas will suck, and that's okay.

- Examine the market by answering these questions:

  - What are the current trends within the writing and publishing industry?
  - Which genres are on the outs?
  - Which genres are making a comeback?
  - Which niches are thriving?
  - Which books are people reading, and why?

- Writing what you want to read will help fuel your passion for the book. Answering these questions will help you:

  - What story calls to you?

- What would you like to see more of in fiction?
- Which idea keeps coming back into your mind throughout the day?

- Passion and marketing should co-exist. When looking at your ideas, ask yourself:

- Which idea is performing best in the current market?
- Which idea would be quicker or easier to write?
- Which idea would suit you best at this stage of your writing journey?

- With that idea in mind, mold that spark into a premise. Most, if not all pieces of fiction revolve around a conflict the main character must overcome or a goal they're fighting to achieve. Naming the conflict or goal of the story will create a short premise, allowing you to tell your story in its simplest terms.

CHAPTER 2
HOW TO STRUCTURE YOUR NOVEL

YES, IT'S THAT IMPORTANT

NOW THAT YOU have an exciting concept to play with, you may be thinking it's time to start outlining—or if you're especially overzealous, writing. I'm going to ask you to sit tight for a minute. Before we dive into the creation process, it's vital to have a proper understanding of story **structure**.

Not only is structure insanely important to the writing process, it's also the part most amateur writers neglect. If you don't structure your idea, you don't have a plot. And if you don't have a plot, you don't have a book. If you don't have a book, then what the hell are we doing here?

Let's start with the basics. What exactly *is* structure?

Structure is the framework of your novel. It pieces your story together, giving it a natural flow and purpose. Think of it like the framework of a house; without it, you'd just have a giant pile of wood, which is pretty useless to anyone other than the local beaver.

Narrative structure functions in the same way. It ensures that the plot points fit together, so there's a beginning, middle, and an end to your finished novel. Sure, if you nix the structure, you may still have a series of interesting scenes, but there's no cohesion or unity—and most importantly, no story.

Let's familiarize ourselves with the most basic view of story structure.

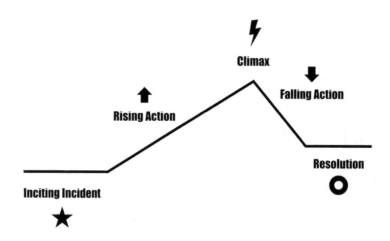

On the left, you have your beginning, or **inciting incident**, which is the event that gets your conflict started.

Climbing up the side of the pyramid is the **rising action**, which is a series of events that further escalates the conflict.

At the tip is the **climax**, which is where your conflict comes to a head.

After the climax, we careen through the **falling action**, then back to even ground for the **resolution**.

Burn this image into your brain. It's going to be the foundation of your novel and literally every piece of fiction you write from this point forward. There are seemingly countless structural options to choose from, but each one of them follows this simple, tried-and-true format.

Now, about those countless structural options. You've probably heard of many of them, and the idea of sifting through them can seem daunting. Don't get caught up in knowing every method or thinking you need to apply all of them to your story. One is not better than another. They all follow the same pattern with different degrees of detail. The key is to find the structure that works best for you.

A few popular structural techniques are the Three-Act Story Structure, the Four-Act Story Structure, the Seven-Point Story Structure, the Mirror Structure, the Hero's Journey, the Heroine's Journey, Save the Cat Beat Sheet, and the W-Plot.

The different techniques range from super-detailed, like the Save the Cat Beat Sheet, while others are vague, like the Mirror Structure.

Here's the bad news: I'm not going to break down every structural method for you. There are entire books devoted to a single structure, let alone dozens, and I'm not trying to release a five-thousand-page tome. If you'd like to study them all (which is unnecessary, but totally your prerogative), I suggest the local library or good ole Google. But for now, I'm giving you a deeper look at three of the more popular structures: the Three-Act Story Structure, the Hero's Journey, and the Heroine's Journey.

THE THREE-ACT STORY STRUCTURE

If you prefer a simpler, more regimented template, the Three-Act Story Structure is a worthy path to explore. It's based off classic three-act plays and divides your novel into parts:

Act 1: The setup

In this act, we establish the characters, the world, and how all these things fit together. Then—*BAM!*—we're hit with the inciting incident that sets the conflict into motion.

Act 2: The confrontation

This act explores the rising action. It's the series of events detailing how the protagonist is trying to fix whatever conflict has arisen, only for things to get progressively worse.

Act 3: The resolution

This is where the climax of the novel happens, the drama is resolved, and the characters discover whatever life lesson they were meant to learn.

THE HERO'S JOURNEY

The Hero's Journey is an extremely popular blueprint specifically for telling a story of heroism, as the name suggests. This template has been around for ages and has cultivated different interpretations and variations over the years, which can be both fascinating and a little overwhelming, depending on how you approach it. On top of that, it's a lot more complicated than some of the other alternatives, as it juggles a Three-Act Story Structure as well as an "ordinary world" and a "special world."

In the teeniest, tiniest nutshell, the Hero's Journey follows a character, the hero, who leaves their ordinary world to go on a quest. The hero meets important characters along the way, and their convictions are tested, until they ultimately defeat the main conflict and return home a changed person.

THE HEROINE'S JOURNEY

I can't mention the Hero's Journey without touching on the Heroine's Journey. This structure has been gaining more notoriety after the release of Gail Carriger's book of the same title. Where the Hero's Journey is about a solo mission to gaining glory, the Heroine's Journey is about cultivating and maintaining community to reach a goal together. To put it simply, while the hero achieves his goal alone, the heroine achieves her goal with allies.

Neither of these "hero" or "heroine" journeys are linked directly to gender, so don't get caught up on the terminology. No matter your protagonist, both structures are valid and worth looking into.

Now that you have the basics, notice each of these templates come down to the fundamental structure in the previous visual: the pyramid. The details and level of depth may vary, but the underlying framework remains the same.

But Jenna . . . do I have to have a story structure?

YES. Have you not been paying attention?

I usually say there are exceptions to any rule, but when it comes to structure, I'm not backing down. If you're writing a fiction novel, it absolutely *has to* have a structure. All plotlines revolve around some kind of conflict or goal, and having a structure ensures the story follows that conflict or goal to completion. Without structure, your book is a series of unrelated events—characters meandering through life, or scenes with no purpose or motivation. That's not a novel.

Remember the pile of wood that dreams of becoming a house? Without a plot, your novel will be the same: an uninteresting pile of words without intention or purpose.

Structure is the epitome of what makes a novel . . . well, a novel. Fortunately, there's good news. The more you write, the more familiar with plotting you'll become, and eventually you won't necessarily have to follow these structures as a rigid guideline. Instead, you'll have the general pyramid memorized, and you might even adopt a method that suits you.

If you were looking at the Three-Act Story Structure, Hero's Journey, or any other template, and didn't feel as though it suited your tastes, there's no need to fret. The more time you devote to writing, the more you develop your own style and voice, and this pertains to story structure as well. It's common for writers to create their own structural method catered specifically to their genre of choice, favorite tropes, or storytelling whims. Of course, these self-made structures still follow the pyramid—we never deviate from that bad boy—but the details are tweaked to fit your style. Sometimes these structures are a hodgepodge of existing templates crammed together, and other times they're an elaboration on the pyramid with particulars noted along the way.

Speaking of which, I have my own structural template I've developed over the years—or decades, if I'm being honest. Like many authors, I studied various structures, then created my own method that enhances my voice. While I typically write within the fantasy and romance genres, nearly all my novels have a few key ingredients: adventure and love stories, to be specific. My structure is designed to fit plots with those core elements.

If you love to write bloody fight scenes and swoon-worthy romance, my structural template might work for you. If your storytelling preferences are nowhere near my tastes, that's fine too. This method still might suit your story, or maybe it won't work at all. I don't know because I don't know a damned thing about your work in progress. What I do know is that examples and insight can only help writers, and at the very least, seeing my personal template may give you ideas for your own.

So, let's have a looksee at my template, shall we?

THE MORECI STRUCTURAL TEMPLATE

ACT 1: THE BEGINNING SHIT[1]

#1 A look into the future. This is not a literal look into the future, but a taste of what the reader should expect later in the book. I suggest evaluating the overall tone of your story and giving your readers a taste of it at the beginning.

For example, if you're writing erotica, you might open with something erotic. Or, if you're writing action-adventure, you might open with a gun fight. I usually start my stories with something violent because my books are often spattered with blood. This gives readers an idea of what they're getting themselves into, plus it opens the story with a genre-appropriate hook.

#2 A look at normal life. This is where we get a look inside our main character's (MC's) version of normal. Maybe they're going to work or handling some daily obligation. Whatever it is, this is their typical day-to-day routine.

It's important to consider that this step should be *brief*. Normal life is boring. We all know what school and work look like, and we don't want it recounted for pages upon pages. A way to skirt around this issue is to showcase the *end* of the main character's day, or only an important snippet of it. Maybe they're clocking out of work or scrawling across the last page of their final exam.

Whatever you do, don't bore readers with a full day of normalcy. The idea is to give them a taste, not lull them to sleep.

#3 Establish desire. What does your MC want or need within their normal life? Find a way to establish this desire, preferably within the step above.

In *The Savior's Champion*, Tobias needs money to care for his struggling family. We see this as he finishes up a day of hard work despite it being a holiday, and then the fact is driven home when he greets his family and sees his mother's exhaustion and his sister's pain.

This step is particularly important. Not only will it make the character's normal life a lot more interesting, but it also sets the stakes. It doesn't matter if the MC's desire ends up changing over the course of the book. That's common, especially if your character experiences a great deal of growth throughout the story. But you should present something missing from their life, or something they're aspiring to achieve. This will help the reader connect with your character on a deeper level while also setting up the conflict and the plot.

#4 Introduce the dilemma. What is the MC's problem? Most of the time, the character's dilemma has a direct relationship to their wants and needs. For example, Tobias *needs* more money to care for his family. What's the issue? He can only get this money by entering the Sovereign's Tournament—a gladiatorial competition that will probably kill him.

Technically, establishing desire and introducing the dilemma can and often do occur at the same time. However, since that isn't always the case, I list them separately for the sake of clarity. Regardless, introducing the dilemma is a major part of Act 1, because it will ultimately trigger the inciting incident.

#5 The MC takes action. And here it is: the inciting incident. The MC decides to take action, or they're thrust into acting on their dilemma by force. Either way, they're taking the first step toward rectifying the situation, which sets the plot into motion.

This is the end of Act 1. The point of this act is to establish the plot. We're creating goals and setting the stakes, we're taking action, and we're letting the readers know what they can expect moving forward.

This act is the shortest within the novel. Personally, I believe it shouldn't last more than four chapters, depending on how you format them. You want to get to the meat of the story in a timely manner.

ACT 2: THE MEAT AND POTATOES

#6 In over their head. At this point, the MC realizes their journey is *way* harder than they expected. They've prepared to tackle their dilemma as best they could, only to realize, *wow . . . this really sucks.*

In *The Savior's Champion*, Tobias enters the labyrinth already afraid for his life, and his fears spike higher as fellow competitors are killed willy-nilly, regardless of the tournament's rules.

This point further strengthens the conflict and the stakes of the story. Additionally, we're establishing that the MC is no longer in their normal world; they are fully engulfed in the conflict, giving them an incentive to do something to get themselves out of this situation and move forward toward their goal.

#7 Blunders. The MC messes up. A lot.

They try to manage their dilemma and fail, perhaps because they're not strong enough, they're not smart enough, they don't know what they're doing, or they need help they don't have or aren't willing to accept. This can be combined with step six, of course, but it doesn't have to be. Just make sure your MC falls flat on their ass a few times before hitting their stride. Remember, stories thrive on conflict, and if the MC's got it too easy, readers aren't going to be motivated to read.

#8 Forced adaptation. Eventually, your MC is going to get sick of failing. Desperate times call for desperate measures, and now they're forced to analyze and adapt to their new environment and struggles. This may include training scenes, befriending allies, or observation; it depends on the story. Essentially, the MC needs to take a potentially painful, embarrassing, or reluctant step toward changing their circumstances, since all their previous attempts were met with disaster.

#9 Their first win. All the learning your character did is finally paying off, and they have their first victory. This could be scoring a coveted interview, gaining the attention of a hunky crush, or besting an opponent in a fight.

In *The Savior's Champion*, Tobias's first win comes when he defeats a terrifying opponent in an arena battle. You can tell this is the case because it happens directly after a series of blunders, a training scene, and accepting assistance.

This win comes at the perfect time because the plot would be a major downer otherwise. Your character has had blunder after blunder, and your entire book cannot be a series of unending failures. You're giving your character a win to prove to both the reader and the MC that there's hope for the future. The end goal, while still intimidating, is just the tiniest bit more achievable.

#10 The perspective shift. This is the start of the MC questioning themselves—who they are, what they want, and where they stand. Secondary characters start viewing them differently. Readers start viewing them differently. Hell, the character probably views themselves differently too.

Some questions or concepts you want to determine within this act are, first and foremost, where are the lines drawn? Who is the MC close with, who are they against, and who is existing in the gray area? Don't give away the answers quite yet. Keep the MC and the readers grappling with these issues.

ACT 3: SHIT GETS WILD

#11 The threat gets a whole lot worse. Your MC just had a win, which means the villain is going to be pissed. Whenever the main character succeeds, you as the writer must raise the stakes. Whatever villain, antagonist, or dilemma your character is facing has to get heated, maybe even as a direct result of their success.

This doesn't have to be a literal villain if you're not writing that kind of story. If you're writing a contemporary romance, it could be that the love interest's ex suddenly shows up and wants their partner back. The idea is to ramp up the conflict so the MC doesn't become complacent after their recent win.

As much as readers cry and complain about the suffering of their favorite characters, no one wants to read a book full of fluff. Smooth sailing is incredibly boring. The goal of this step is to make sure the character's win doesn't last too long and the stakes become even more dire.

#12 The struggle bus. It's not enough to tell the readers the villain is angry, or the ex-girlfriend is in town—they need to see the ramifications in action. At this point, the MC struggles to manage the worsening threat, facing blow after blow. There may be some wins sprinkled along the way, but they're getting harder to achieve, and the threat is weighing heavily on your MC.

#13 The major loss. This could mean a literal loss, as in losing a bet, a challenge, or a match. It could be the loss of a loved one, the injury of a friend, or any other downfall that fits your story. Ultimately, something terrible happens to your MC. This loss is pivotal to the storyline, because it's going to be a catalyst to the next step, which happens to be one of the most important plot points in your novel.

#14 The breaking point. This is the lowest point for the MC. They've suffered a major loss, and now they're not feeling so confident. They're questioning their beliefs, capabilities, allies, or all of the above. This usually causes them to make shitty decisions, like acting in self-sabotaging ways, isolating themselves, or regressing to their old, less seasoned self.

The breaking point doesn't have to be the lowest moment in the MC's life, but it *does* need to be their lowest moment in the novel. This will be the first time the reader sees this character in such emotional turmoil. It's a brand-new low for the MC, and you need this moment because it'll make the high of the climax that much sweeter.

Sometimes the major loss and the breaking point are one and the same. If they're not, they usually happen in rapid succession. Perhaps the major loss occurs in Chapter 20, whereas the breaking point happens in Chapter 21.

#15 The wallow. Remember that emotional turmoil I mentioned? This is it. Your MC has found themselves in a messy situation, and they're wallowing. That's not to say they're being a whiney, stinky mess, but they're suffering from the consequences of their breaking point. They may be feeling grief, remorse, anger, or self-hatred. They may even be accepting failure and giving up altogether.

No one bounces back from a breaking point overnight, and your MC should be no different. While this point doesn't need to be lengthy, it helps add realism to the story while making the resolution feel even more unreachable.

#16 The redemption. Your character crawls out of their pit of despair and decides to redeem themselves. The key here is to give them *a reason* for their redemption. Usually, it has something to do with having one last chance to achieve their goal, or maybe seeing that situations are especially dire and they're truly the only person who can save the day. They need to shake off their funk, right their wrongs, and seize glory. More importantly, they need to make the decision for themselves.

#17 The almost. This moment usually happens right before or during the climax. We're nearing the end of the story, and the MC faces the threat, villain, or dilemma head-on . . . and *almost* loses. I mean *really* loses. Like, as losery as it can possibly get. If the stakes are low, then maybe they miss the train to reunite with their love interest. If the stakes are high, then it probably means your poor, beaten down MC almost dies.

This moment is pivotal to any effective climax. No one values a success story that came easily. Watching the hero crush their opponent without breaking a sweat isn't inspiring. In fact, it's a bit obnoxious. We want to see people struggle because struggle is something most people can relate to. The almost provides that. It's that moment before or during the climax when the MC feels most vulnerable, and thus most relatable and human.

#18 The climax. Congratulations, you've reached the apex of your novel. This is the pinnacle of the story—the moment when all the obstacles come to a head. The MC is directly facing their conflict or goal, and their actions and reactions will determine whether they win or lose. Of course, nine times out of ten they're going to win, or at least partially.

Again, the almost will likely occur right before or during the climax. Doing so ensures the win doesn't come too easily, which will make the inevitable victory even more glorious. The idea is to lay on the tension and drama. You are finally resolving the big dilemma one way or another, and you're not making it easy on your character or your readers.

#19 The fallout. Typically, the climax of a novel can be very revealing. It unveils secrets or exposes hidden agendas and lies. The fallout is when the characters regroup to ask questions and provide explanations.

This point tends to be a dialogue-heavy moment. That's fine as long as the conversations flow naturally, and you're not making readers sit through too much exposition. We get it—the MC has questions, and so does the reader! You're welcome to answer them, just get to the point.

Pro tip: If you're writing a series, not every question should be answered. If every question *is* answered, more questions need to be revealed. That way readers have incentive to pick up the next book and further explore the mystery.

#20 The resolution. Finally, the reader can relax—well, sometimes. The resolution is when at least one main problem of the story is resolved. If this is a standalone novel, then most of the dilemmas should be put to rest. If it's a series, you can resolve an issue or two, but leave something huge on the table for future novels.

Resolutions are wonderful because they can evoke satisfaction, rage, or an eagerness to read more. It all depends on what you're going for. A resolution can be as simple as a kiss between lovers or as complex as a peace treaty between planets.

With the resolution, Act 3 of our novel is complete. You focused on the MC's exploration of self as well as their confusion regarding their beliefs and integrity. Maybe they're not so sure about the path they've chosen or who they want to be. But ultimately, the act will end in some semblance of self-acceptance. They will finally feel at peace with their choices, at least to some degree, and that provides a resolution for both them and the reader.

If my structural method intrigues you, feel free to examine it. If it isn't your thing, then build your own. That's the beauty of being a writer; we have the power to destroy and create however we please.

Right now, you should have an idea of what structure your story should take on. Once you've nailed down the framework of your plot, we can move on to the planning phase, where we flesh out our characters, organize our ideas, and most importantly, outline our novel.

---

1. If you wanted proper names, you came to the wrong place.

SUMMARY

HOW TO STRUCTURE YOUR NOVEL

- Familiarize yourself with the most basic view of story structure: the pyramid. Print, copy, or draw it out and place it near your workspace.

- Even though there are countless structural options to choose from, each follows the simple, tried-and-true format—inciting incident, rising action, climax, falling action, and resolution.

- None of the structural methods are better than the rest, but you should find one that works for you.

- The Three-Act Story Structure:

- *Act 1: the setup.* Establish the characters, the world, and how they fit together. Hit your reader with the inciting incident that sets the conflict into motion.
- *Act 2: the confrontation.* This act explores the rising action. Show how your protagonist is trying to fix whatever conflict has arisen only for things to get progressively worse.
- *Act 3: the resolution.* This is where the climax of the novel happens, the drama is resolved, and the characters discover whatever life lesson they were meant to learn.

- The Hero's Journey follows a character, the hero, who leaves their ordinary world to go on a quest. The hero meets important characters along the way, and their convictions are tested until they ultimately defeat the main conflict and return home a changed person.

- The Heroine's Journey is about cultivating and maintaining community to reach a goal together.

- The Moreci Structural Template:

- Act 1: The Beginning Shit
- *A look into the future.* This is a taste of what the reader should expect later in the book, while opening with a genre-appropriate hook.
- *A look at normal life.* This is where we get a brief look inside our main character's version of normal.
- *Establish desire*: What does your main character want or need?
- *Introduce the dilemma.* Most of the time, the character's dilemma has a direct relationship to their wants and needs.
- *The MC takes action.* The MC makes a decision to take action, or they're thrust into acting on their dilemma.
- Act 2: The Meat and Potatoes
- *In over their head.* The MC realizes they are no longer in their normal world and are fully engulfed in the conflict, giving them an incentive to get themselves out of this situation and move forward toward their goal.
- *Blunders.* The MC tries to manage their dilemma and fails.
- *Forced adaptation.* Your MC is forced to analyze and adapt to their new environment and struggles.
- *Their first win.* The MC's effort finally pays off, and they have their first victory.
- *The perspective shift.* The MC starts to question themselves, who they are, what they want, and where they stand.
- Act 3: Shit Gets Wild
- *The threat gets a whole lot worse.* Whatever villain, antagonist, or dilemma your character is facing gets heated, maybe even as a direct result of their success.

- *The struggle bus.* The MC struggles to manage the worsening threat, facing blow after blow.
- *The major loss.* Something terrible happens to your MC.
- *The breaking point.* This is the lowest point for the MC.
- *The wallow.* Your MC has found themselves in a messy situation, and they're wallowing.
- *The redemption.* Your character crawls out of their pit of despair and decides to redeem themselves.
- *The almost.* The MC faces the threat, villain, or dilemma head-on and *almost* loses.
- *The climax.* The MC is directly facing their conflict or goal, and their actions and reactions will determine whether they win or lose.
- *The fallout.* The characters regroup to ask questions and provide explanations.
- *The resolution.* At least one main problem of the story is resolved. If this is a standalone novel, then most of the dilemmas should be put to rest. If it's a series, then leave something big and intriguing for future novels.

CHAPTER 3
PLANNING YOUR NOVEL
LAYING THE GROUNDWORK FOR SUCCESS

WITH THE STRUCTURE from Chapter 2 in mind, it's time to fill in the gaping holes of your story's framework with all the exciting, twisted, and magical stuff you can concoct.

Don't get too excited; we're not writing the book quite yet because first we need to give our imagination space to shine. This is the time for brainstorming the most important aspects of your novel.

Thought dump

But Jenna, what the hell is a thought dump?

It's commonly referred to as brainstorming, but I think the term *thought dumping* creates a more accurate visual. Your mind is dumping out ideas, and some of those ideas are going to be shit.

This is a vital part of my creative process, and I highly recommend you make it a part of yours as well.

Thought dumping is simple; take all your ideas for your story and write them down. World-building, characters, plot points, physical descriptions, whatever. This step is uncomplicated, unrestricted, and entirely creative. Consider this your opportunity to get your thoughts out—and I mean *any* thoughts. Streams of dialogue, fight choreographies, even sex scenes.

Write. It. Down.

There really is no right or wrong way to thought dump. You're literally just writing out every single idea that comes to mind regarding your story. It doesn't matter if the ideas suck, nor does it matter if they are in sequential order. You'll worry about that later.

For now, ignore your inhibitions, and let the ideas flow freely.

Now, where should you put these ideas? This is the time to pick your poison. Some writers thought dump in physical notebooks, others use a simple Word document or a Google Doc, and plenty use a note-taking app on their phone for thought dumping on the go. Another popular option is Milanote, a platform for organizing and brainstorming. You could also try Novelpad, a writing software designed specifically with novelists in mind.

No matter where you store these ideas, cherish them and keep them safe —that means hit the *save* button, if you weren't sure. You're going to reference your thought dump frequently, possibly even long after your story is complete.

Character creation, world-building, and outlining

But Jenna, this seems like a lot for one step.

It is. In fact, if you read the Table of Contents, you'll notice there's an entire chapter devoted to each of these elements.

I'm listing them as the same step because I highly recommend working on these items concurrently. As much as I would love to streamline the writing process, these particular elements are intertwined. By looking at them side by side, you'll decrease your chances of plot holes, writer's block, and needing rewrites.

Your characters' strengths and weaknesses need to enhance your plot, the plot's conflicts need to fit into the world you've built, the intricacies of your world need to make sense for the characters you've created, and look at that, we're back to square one.

You hear all the time about writers who spend years building a world only to realize they can't think of a single plot to suit it. Same with building characters despite having no story to plop them into. This is why you *must* create these elements together.

But we need to define things in order to understand them, right?

Character creation is essential from the start. Who is the main player and who are the people who support or thwart them? All of your characters need to serve a purpose in the story; if they don't have one, give them the boot.

World-building is important as well. You can't have your characters wandering through whitespace. You need to spark life into your book and the readers' minds with a rich world for your characters to inhabit.

Think about the large and small details of the world and everything in between that is important to your characters' story. This can include magic systems, geography, history, technology, and so much more.

This concept is important for all stories, though it plays a much larger role in some genres versus others. Regardless, whether you're creating an entirely new planet or a small town in Alaska, you've got to at least have a firm grasp on the setting your characters are traveling through.

With the "who" and "where" of your story covered, now we need to know the "what." What is your story about? That's where the outline comes in.

An **outline** is like a blueprint for your book. It breaks down the events that are going to occur, and it details them in sequential order. This serves as a guide for you to reference so you can ensure your story's unfolding according to plan.

Remember that thought dump we talked about?

This is why we took that step: to enrich your characters, your world-building, and your outline.

Don't worry about all that during the thought dumping phase. Remember, the whole point is to come up with as much content as possible. But once we've got that content at the ready, it'll serve as much-needed fodder for planning our story.

Until then, create. Have fun with it. Tap into an inspiring playlist or Pinterest board and let the ideas flow. The heftier your thought dump, the better prepared you'll be when you start outlining.

Tense and point of view

Knowing your tense and point of view before writing will help you establish the lens of your story. You need to pick one of each—even for stories with multiple points of view—and stick with it.

When it comes to **tense** in fiction, past and present tense are the most popular, which is why I'll focus on them throughout this book.

Past tense refers to when the story is told through the retelling of past events. Present tense, as you can probably guess, focuses on events happening right now in the character's life.

When it comes to **point of view**, we're looking at the narration of the book—the voice through which the readers are hearing, seeing, and learning the events of the story.

The two most popular points of view in fiction are first person and third person. Most of the time, the pronouns used will highlight which point of view the reader is experiencing the story through.

When it comes to tense and point of view, no choice is wrong per se, but you need to be consistent, or you'll confuse the hell out of your readers.

Now that you've dumped your thoughts out, let's get to planning your story, starting with creating your characters.

SUMMARY

PLANNING YOUR NOVEL

- Thought dump every idea about your story that you have, including characters, plot points, and world-building.

  - Choose a medium you prefer: a notebook, Word, Google Docs, Milanote, Novelpad, a note-taking app, etc.
  - Write down everything you know about the story—without any worries regarding how "good" these ideas are.
  - Be creative in this process. You might not keep all these ideas, but this is the time for your imagination to shine.

- Character creation, world-building, and outlining should occur concurrently.

- Consider the tense and point of view of your story, and stick with the one you pick.

CHAPTER 4
CHARACTER CREATION

CRAFTING YOUR BAND OF MISFITS

COUNTLESS WRITERS HAVE TOLD me they struggle with creating characters. They end up flat, unrealistic, one-dimensional —or in one word, boring.

I'm going to help you with that.

Even if you believe you're writing the best character in the world, it's pivotal to brush up on this skill set. No matter how rich the world is or how riveting the plot is, lifeless characters will drag a story down and potentially ruin it altogether. You want your cast to captivate your readers and pull them along for the ride, and I'm here to give you the tools to make that happen.

First, let's define the types of characters that will inhabit your story.

The **protagonist** is the main character. They drive the story forward, and usually the reader is following their journey.

The **antagonist** is the main opposition to your protagonist. Often, they're a **villain** with evil intentions to thwart your protagonist's journey, but not always. A villain is an antagonist, but an antagonist isn't necessarily a villain.

The **love interest** plays the role as, you guessed it, the lover of the main character. In a romance novel, the love interest can also be one of the protagonists. In any other genre, the love interest is usually a supporting character.

Supporting characters are characters ranging from the best friend of the protagonist to the unnamed postal worker your main character meets for a single line in the first chapter, never to be seen again.

There are more character types, such as deuteragonist, confidante, foil, and several others, but we're starting with the basics here. If you'd like to dig a little deeper, the internet is vast and informative, albeit weird. Tread lightly.

Now that we have the general definitions out of the way, let's go through some tips for writing realistic, believable characters who your readers can relate to.

GIVE 'EM DIMENSION

People are three-dimensional, so your characters should be as well. Otherwise, none of your readers will relate to them.

I cringe whenever someone says, "*this* character is the comic relief" or "*this* character is the damsel in distress." Sometimes we generalize for the sake of brevity, but if you're genuinely writing your characters in this format—with only one personality type in mind—I promise, your readers won't buy it.

Real people, even the shallowest ones, have dimensions. None of us exist exclusively to fulfill a single expectation. We each have strengths, weaknesses, talents, and insecurities. These are things you should be fleshing out in your characters, alongside their wants, desires, fears, and quirks.

Sometimes writers overthink this step. Sure, their character is intelligent, grumpy, and a little insecure, but now the writer is convinced they need to tack on twenty more personality traits to make their character stand out. First of all, calm down. Yes, people have multiple traits, but if uniqueness is your goal, this ain't the way to achieve it. After all, lots of people are funny, cowardly, or horny—nothing about that is unique. When adding dimension to your character, it's important to consider the little things—the traits, however small, that make your characters distinctive.

For example, is your character multilingual? Maybe their English—or whichever language your story is written in—isn't perfect because it's not their native tongue.

Is your character a warrior? Maybe they have exposed scars from years of battle.

Is your character younger than the rest of the cast? Maybe they speak with age-appropriate slang the others find silly or confusing.

You'll notice that none of these examples are personality traits, but every single one of them makes the character appear different, however slight, from the others. This is one of my favorite parts of character creation because you get to add something special to each of your characters.

REALISM

Even if you're writing sci-fi with creatures from another universe, you need to craft a story your readers will connect to. Readers want to escape into a book and possibly see themselves.

A lot of writers craft their characters and go with what they believe is the default: a cisgender straight character, usually male, though females sometimes make the list. They're white, conventionally attractive, have a slender or athletic build, have no physical disabilities or mental illnesses of any kind, and they're neurotypical.

I'm sure this person exists, but I've yet to meet anyone who fits this description.

Even if we look at people who tick a lot of these boxes, you'll usually find at least one outlier. My partner is a cishet, conventionally attractive white man, but he is physically disabled due to a spinal cord injury. And a lot of people look like they might check all the boxes, but you can't see their queerness, mixed heritage, neurodivergence, or hidden illness.

What's my point? This world is a big mashup of different kinds of people, and if you aren't taking these factors into consideration, you're not writing realistic characters. It's not believable that your entire cast looks the same, acts the same, and experiences life in the same way—unless you're writing about clones, but even that would be a stretch. Your story may not take place in our world, but the readers still need to believe it could conceivably exist, which means writing characters who are as varied as the people in the world we live in.

Now, just because you create a world filled with rich and diverse characters doesn't mean you have to info dump. A lot of new writers believe that in order to create realistic characters, they need to tell readers every detail about them, like their backstory, their deepest scars, every thought and emotion, and that one time they got a hand job in the back of a movie theater.

Yes, it's helpful to know all this information, as it will allow you to craft their voice and actions in a realistic manner. And yes, sometimes this information is pivotal to the plot—well, maybe not the hand job. But *pivotal* is the keyword here. If the details don't enhance the story, paint a picture, or drive the plot forward, they can stay in your imagination where they belong.

For example, it's always useful to list a character's skin color. Skin is the largest organ on the human body, and it allows the reader to visualize the character. Without it, they're just an amorphous blob. But we don't need to know the details of their tragic childhood unless it's playing a direct role in their character arc. Villain origin story, anyone?

In *The Savior's Champion*, the main character, Tobias, had a strained relationship with his father. I didn't mention it in the book because it was never relevant.

Gather all the information you can about your character, but choose the appropriate moments to reveal these tidbits, and be honest about whether certain details need to be revealed at all.

BALANCE THE POSITIVE AND THE NEGATIVE

It's human nature to be flawed beyond comprehension, so if your character is only good and kind, then roll up your sleeves, because you've got some work to do. Nobody is just one thing, and your readers will be able to sniff out a phony character before the second page.

Give your character depth by balancing out their kindness with a streak of stealing from the local farmer's market. Sure, they're doing it to feed their kids, but it makes the character more dynamic and can reveal a lot about their moral compass. In turn, this can help escalate or even cause conflicts, which only makes the reading experience more compelling.

Now, the scale doesn't necessarily have to be even. You can tip it toward either side, depending on the role of the character; your lead will probably need more likable than unlikeable traits, and an effective villain should probably be a massive dick. But no one should be wholly virtuous or one hundred percent scum, snot, and everything putrid. Throw a dash of spice in there, and your readers will thank you.

ASK AND OBSERVE

One of the most common questions I hear about writing characters is, how do I write [insert character type here]? In situations like these, writers are looking for a formula. Just add a drop of this trait and a dash of that cliché, and behold, you've written a pile of shit.

These hopeful writers overlook the obvious. You are around people every day of your life. Even if you're a recluse, like me, I'm sure you watch them on television and in movies, or communicate with them on the internet.

Observe them.

We live in a big world filled with lots of people. I know, I hate it too. But if we have to exist among them, we might as well learn something about them. If you want your character to be redeemable, what do you find redeemable among humankind? If you want them to be likable, what do you personally like in a fellow human being?

It's really that simple.

Stop trying to overcomplicate realism. If you're searching for a step-by-step format, you're doing it wrong.

See people. Talk to people. Pay attention to what you like and what you dislike. Experience is one of the biggest assets to your writing. Utilize it.

This is when I drop the turd on you: Your experience has limits. That is why we ask others to read our stories and weigh in. Whether these people are editors, beta readers, critique partners, or sensitivity readers, you need someone else to look at your characters, especially if you're writing outside of your own life experience. We'll dive deeper into this topic in Chapters 24 and 25.

But, Jenna, aren't these people going to steal my brilliant ideas?

They don't want to steal them. Ideas are a dime a dozen, and yours are no more special than the next.

But what if they don't like how I portrayed my characters?

Then fix it, you silly goose.

Wouldn't you rather know your characters suck before publication as opposed to after? That way you can have a good cry and then edit your book.

And no, not all outside opinions will be correct. Like we already covered, people are inherently flawed. But that's why we have multiple people read our work, and we look for trends within the feedback.

And I'm not talking about having your best friend, mom, or girlfriend read your story. Enlist readers who don't care about you and are totally comfortable tearing you to shreds.

You're welcome.

CHARACTER PROFILE

Now that you've unlocked the keys to writing layered, realistic characters, we're going to dive deeper. If you know your characters inside and out, it's going to be a lot easier to write them.

A character profile is exactly what it sounds like: an outline of your character, detailing every facet of their appearance, personality, and lifestyle. You can—and should—list all of their valuable traits, including their culture and race, belief system, darkest fears, and everything in between.

But Jenna, do I need to create a profile for all *of my characters?*

That guy who shows up to deliver two lines of exposition probably doesn't need a character profile. Neither does the dad who dies at the start of the first chapter. As for your other, more prominent characters, that's up to you. In my opinion, if the character is a regularly occurring member of the cast, it doesn't hurt to make a profile. Remember, this is all about making the writing process easier for you. The better you know your characters, the more seamless their dialogue, actions, and reactions will be.

And because I'm a merciful writer, I'm not going to leave you high and dry. Here's a look at my personal character profile setup, including the bare minimum of traits you should consider.

A couple of things to keep in mind. One, just because you're listing these traits doesn't mean they need to go into your novel. This process is to help you get to know your character so you can easily write them, not so you can stuff a laundry list of useless information into your story. And two, consider this format modifiable. There are plenty of other traits you can add to your personal character profile. I've seen profiles with more than one hundred categories to fill out. No, that's not a typo. I'm not listing that many things, because I have books to write. Consider this a starting point.

CHARACTER PROFILE TEMPLATE

BASIC STATS

Sex and gender. Keep in mind, sex and gender are not the same thing. Sex is biological, whereas gender is a societal construct. If your story takes place in a fictional world, the idea of gender may be different from ours.

Age. Think about this one carefully because age plays a huge role in a character's life experience, and life experience can completely transform someone's personality. Additionally, the age of your main characters can dictate the category of your novel. For example, if you're aiming to write a young adult novel, then your main characters absolutely must be between the ages of 14 and 19.

Race, ethnicity, and culture. These are important to consider for a multitude of reasons. Race or ethnicity can help guide the character's physical description. Depending on the society, these traits can unfortunately dictate privilege or treatment within your novel's world. Some people contribute a lot of their identity to their ethnicity and culture, and even fictional worlds have countries or realms. Your characters must have some kind of lineage. It could be Cuban. It could be Elven. It could be Class 21Q from the Planet ZoopKnob. Figure it out.

Physical appearance. I recommend all writers nail down these physical traits at an absolute minimum: **skin color**; **eye color**; **hair color**, **length**, and **texture**; **height**; and **body type**. It's also a good idea to think of any unique, defining physical traits. For example, in *The Savior's Series*, Tobias's eyes are such a dark shade of brown, they're often mistaken for black. Leila has a freckle below her left eye, Kaleo has a series of scars across both his arms, and Raphael has dimples.

This is also a great time to determine how your character's appearance affects them. Have you ever met a supremely gorgeous person who was also supremely arrogant? I'm sure you have. But keep in mind that a person's appearance doesn't have to dictate their personality. Just because a character's small doesn't mean they're sweet or weak, and just because they're large and unkempt doesn't mean they're dumb and brutish.

Location. Where is your character from? Where do they live? And I'm talking specifics. Country, state, town, and residence. You also want to know what their lifestyle is like. Are they rich? Are they poor? Are they coasting? Are they struggling? These details often play a huge role in personality and experience. Someone from a small town with minimal amenities is going to have a wildly different perspective on life than a socialite from a big city.

RELATIONSHIPS

Family. What's their family like? How's their relationship with their family members? Maybe their dad's an abusive piece of shit. Maybe their mom has a drinking problem. The number one thing that messes up a person is their family, so digging through a character's genealogy is a great way to reveal their insecurities and issues.

Friends. A person's friendships can also say a lot about them. If you're hanging out with a bunch of jerks, you're probably a jerk too. And as the story progresses, your character's friendships might change. Maybe their pals abandon them in their time of need, or maybe your character simply outgrows them.

Sexual orientation. Please keep in mind that there are a lot of sexual orientations to choose from. If you can only think of a couple, you're slacking. Asexual, homosexual, heterosexual, bisexual, pansexual, graysexual, omnisexual . . . Have I lost you yet? Then it's time to do some research.

Sexual and romantic attraction. I combined these two for the sake of brevity, but please understand these are very different experiences. Sexual attraction is what makes your bits tingle, whereas romantic attraction is what makes your heart flutter.

Take a look at your character. What are they into? Just because they're sexually attracted to men doesn't mean they're attracted to *all* men. Maybe a defined six-pack gets them riled up, but a goofball sends their heart racing. Maybe they don't experience sexual or romantic attraction at all. Have fun with this part.

Experience. Just because your character likes dicks doesn't mean they've touched one. Not only do I like to determine a character's sexual history, but I also like to determine why that's the case. Why are they a player? Why are they celibate?

This is also a great time to determine your character's romantic experience as well. Have they ever been in a relationship? Hell, have they ever been on a date? Have they had their heart broken, or have they never fallen in love in the first place?

APTITUDE

Skills. What is your character good at, and how did they develop these skills? If your character is your average teen nerd in one chapter, but in the next they're single handedly fighting off werewolves, you'll have to be able to rationalize this. No one is suddenly an expert at something—unless it's magic, which may very well be the reason.

Occupation or schooling. Are they good at school? Do they like their job? Most people don't. Why is that the case for this character?

Hobbies. What does your character do when they're not killing aliens or casting spells? This may not come up often in most speculative fiction, but if you're writing contemporary, hobbies tend to be very useful when creating bonding moments between characters.

PERSONALITY AND CHARACTER

Introvert, extrovert, or a little of both? Is your character an introvert or an extrovert? Most people qualify as ambiverts, which is a middle ground between the two extremes. But it's still a good idea to figure out if your character leans toward one side more than the other. Remember, an introvert isn't necessarily shy, and an extrovert isn't necessarily brazen. Introverts gain energy from being alone, whereas extroverts gain energy from being around people.

Strengths and weaknesses. This is pivotal, especially for your most important characters, as their strengths and weaknesses are going to fuel the plot. If a character's ambitious, that could be a major strength. If they're ambitious to the point of disregarding the feelings of their loved ones, that could be a major weakness, or even the cause of their downfall. If your character is a good guy, you want to know what makes them heroic and what makes them human. If they're a bad guy, you want to know what makes them formidable and what makes them falter.

Goals, dreams, and aspirations. What is your character striving for, and do these aspirations change over the course of the novel? It's actually very common for a character's goals to change as the story progresses, especially if the character in question is the protagonist.

Beliefs and affiliations. Most people believe in something. It could be a simple code of ethics, a religion, science, or a combination of these things. Does your character have a sense of duty or purpose? Do they believe in right and wrong? If so, what do they think constitutes right and wrong?

Fears and insecurities. To write a compelling story, your characters need to have some legitimate fears and insecurities. Maybe they're insecure about their future. Maybe they're afraid of losing their sense of self. Some books have life-and-death stakes, so being afraid to die is a very valid fear. However, you'll probably need something deeper and more relatable to hook the reader. In doing this, you're determining the root of your character's vulnerability, and this is vital to crafting a realistic character.

Who or what would they die for? Someone's about to fire a gun. What would compel your character to run in front of that bullet? This allows you to tap into the heart and soul of your character. You learn a lot about a person when you determine what it is they truly care about.

As I said, these are just a few things to consider when creating a character profile. Do you think I missed anything? Then be sure to add it to your own list. I encourage you to look online for examples and interpretations. Remember, this is about making the writing process as easy as possible, and that means catering it to what works best for you.

SUMMARY
CHARACTER CREATION

- Define your characters:

  - Protagonist
  - Antagonist
  - Love interest
  - Supporting characters

- For each of these characters:

  - What are their three-dimensional qualities: strengths, weaknesses, talents, insecurities, etc.?
  - How are they realistic?
  - What are their positive and negative traits?
  - Enlist the help of critique partners, beta readers, and editors when crafting your characters.

- Build a character profile by listing the following traits for each of your main and supporting characters:

  - Sex and gender
  - Age

- Race, ethnicity, and culture
- Physical appearance
- Skin color; eye color; hair color, length, and texture; height; and body type
- Location
- Family
- Friends
- Sexual orientation
- Sexual and romantic attraction
- Experience
- Overall skills
- Occupation or schooling
- Hobbies
- Introvert, extrovert, or ambivert?
- Strengths and weaknesses
- Goals, dreams, and aspirations
- Beliefs and affiliations
- Fears and insecurities
- Who or what would they die for?

CHAPTER 5
WORLD-BUILDING

A WHOLE NEW WORLD . . . OR MAYBE JUST MORE OF THE SAME

AS MENTIONED IN CHAPTER 3, world-building means creating the setting of your wonderous story. No matter what genre you're writing or the locations involved, be it a faraway planet or the streets of San Francisco, your story will require at least some amount of world-building. The details of the world will make the plot more vivid for the reader, transporting them into the story so they can experience it alongside your characters. And while you will certainly need to spend more time building a fictional kingdom as opposed to an already existing Caribbean Island, there are virtually no situations where a writer can skip this step.

If you're in the thought dump stage, naming anything and everything you can think up is a great idea; let's keep those creative juices flowing. But if you're having trouble with the idea of creating an entire world, start off with only the details relevant to your characters and their immediate needs.

In this chapter, I'm giving you a world-building template as well as some world-building tips to make the path that much smoother.

WORLD-BUILDING TEMPLATE

SETTING

Overall setting. Where does your novel take place? Depending on your story, this could cover an entire globe, or it could be relegated to a single village. For example, the world you created could be called Cyborgia, but your story takes place specifically in Jennalea, Kingdom of Moresica. Pretty awesome names if I do say so myself.

World. As in the planet that houses your setting. What is it called? Maybe it's another plane of existence. Maybe it's a world floating in the sky high above the clouds. Or maybe you're writing within a contemporary setting, which means the planet is Earth.

Continents, countries, and kingdoms. Take a metaphorical pizza cutter to that planet you just created. Once you've divided it, give each slice a name. You don't have to name every country or kingdom, but you should at least name the ones relevant to your story.

Villages, cities, and towns. I'm sticking with the pizza analogy even though it's making me hungry. What toppings make up those countries and kingdoms? Those are your smaller divisions. If they're applicable to your story, name them. Of course, if you're writing in a contemporary setting, this may be as simple as researching the various cities that make up the Bay Area of California, or creating a fictional town in southern Louisiana.

Flora and climate. We're getting into nature. The easiest thing to nail down is the weather. Is your setting scorching? Is it snowy? Similarly, you want to consider the seasons, because not all places experience a traditional spring, summer, fall, and winter. And of course, all that sunshine and rain is going to have a direct effect on the trees, grass, and flowers—or lack thereof.

The earth. I'm using this term loosely, since your setting might not even take place on planet Earth. Basically, point your eyes downward. What does the ground look like? Is everything mud or dirt? Maybe it's desert sand. Maybe there's paved or cobblestone roads. Maybe there isn't any ground at all, in which case, grab hold of something quick before you plummet to your death.

Animal life. Perhaps your lush green forests are filled with hopping bunnies and frolicking deer. Maybe your hot pink jungles are slithering with poisonous snake-monsters. Depending on how fantastical your story is, this is a great place to let your imagination run wild—pun intended.

Architecture. We're breaking this down with three questions: Where do people live, what do the buildings look like, and what are they made of? Be sure the architecture fits the climate and setting. A barren desert probably isn't going to boast large wooden homes unless they have substantial trade agreements.

History. This is where a lot of writers get sucked into the never-ending world-building abyss. Before you get started, be honest with yourself. How much of your world history do you actually *need* in order to tell the story? About 75 percent of the time, all you need to focus on are the defining moments. How was the kingdom born or created, and how did the current government or leader come into power?

Keep in mind, history is messy. The neater and more orderly you make your world's backstory, the less believable it's going to be.

SOCIETY

Politics and government. What's your setting's system of government? Is it a monarchy? A democracy? An oligarchy? Who is the most powerful person or people in this world and why? How are laws passed and enforced? Is there a military? Is there a judicial system? Is there a monetary system? Prisons? Punishment? Death penalty? Public torture? This one's a doozy, and in certain genres, it may not be necessary. But if you're writing about alien soldiers or magical kings and queens, you're writing about politics, and it's time to flesh out those details.

Class systems. Is there an upper, middle, and lower class? Is everyone equal, or is there a caste system? An unfortunate reality of many societies is the existence of hierarchies, so give this one some thought when building your world.

Racial groups. Are there particular ethnicities or races that are more common in your setting, or is it evenly mixed? Why is this the case? Remember, if immigration is possible in your world, it's perfectly believable for your setting to boast all kinds of characters.

Gender norms and expectations. It's very common for writers to include the same gender norms that we have in the real world or try to mirror norms from past civilizations. These are reasonable possibilities, but sometimes it isn't believable. Why would a completely different world have none of our customs but all of our gender norms? A lot of writers don't thoroughly research gender throughout history and go with incorrect generalizations; don't fall into this trap.

Prejudices and discrimination. Like the previous section, this is something a lot of writers try to base off "history" without doing proper homework. Reading classic fantasy novels does not count as a history lesson. If your world mirrors a bygone era, do some thorough research before diving into the writing process.

Sexual orientation. How is it viewed? Is sexuality a social identifier? It hasn't always been that way. This is another situation where researching history can be your friend, especially if your world is based on a historical society.

Children. How are they raised? How are they treated? How are they expected to behave? What's the normal number of children to have?

Education and careers. Break down how schooling works in your world, if it exists at all, and what sort of jobs are available, respected, and coveted. Additionally, when are people expected to transition from school to work? Is this based on age or class?

Societal expectations or norms. While this entire section covers society, there are plenty of other norms that might fit into your story. Explore which expectations your world might enforce, regardless of whether they meet the aforementioned qualifiers.

CULTURE

Belief systems and customs. Does your world have some type of belief system? What about holidays, celebrations, or unique cultural customs? This could tie directly into your world's beliefs, like Christmas, for example. Or your world could have holidays and parties that are historically based, like President's Day.

Romance. How are relationships treated? What about dating, sex, or marriage? Is PDA frowned upon? Is sex liberal and free? Are there any romantic expectations at all? In some societies, people are expected to get married very young, or marriage is treated like a business transaction rather than a romantic declaration.

Arts. This covers music, dancing, writing, theater, and all forms of visual art. Is this a thing in your world? If it is, what's it like? If not, why?

Sports, athletics, and entertainment. What sort of sports exist? Do they involve jousting on horseback, or fighting to the death for sheer entertainment? Speaking of entertainment, what's that like in your world? What do people do for fun?

Clothing, accessories, or body modifications. Are tattoos and piercings a thing? Do people color their hair? Do people wear underwear? Is clothing gendered, class-based, or solely functional? Do low-rise jeans exist? If so, what did your characters do to deserve such torture?

Ethics. What are some moral codes people typically follow? This could be related to your religious system, or it could have nothing to do with it. Maybe honor is just an extremely important concept in your world, or among a certain race of people within your setting.

Technology, science, and magic. I combine these things because they often go together. For example, sometimes science heals people, but other times it's the result of technology, and in some stories it's all about magic. You need to figure out the extent of your world's technological advancements, their knowledge of science, and their magic system, if they have one at all. Nail down as many details as you can: the capabilities, the limitations, who has access to it, and who doesn't.

This template is not an exhaustive list. There are plenty more available on the vast interwebs with too many categories to count. Utilize this list for your own writing, or let it be a starting point before you research additives.

Knowing exactly *what* to build isn't all it takes to properly create a setting. There are quite a few missteps writers make when world-building, and unfortunately, these blunders are all too common. Here are some extra tips to help you marry your world with your story without putting off readers.

AVOID THE INFO DUMP

It's great to figure out the history of your world. You'll need to know the details about its government, foreign relations, and class system, because this will allow you to easily blend your setting into your story. But your readers don't need to know every single facet of your world, and they certainly don't need to know it all at once in a massive info dump.

A lot of world-builders, especially fantasy and sci-fi writers, like to include a multipage info dump at the start of the story. This stinky pile lists every minute detail of their world, down to the legal system and imports and exports. Let me put it to you plainly: This is boring. Sure, sometimes exposition is necessary, but sparingly and in small doses.

Instead of inserting paragraphs about the climate, the reader will understand the setting is cold when your characters are trudging through snow. You don't need to explain the class system when your character is referring to some people as nobles and others as peasants. Allow your audience to experience the world as the characters journey through the story. This reads a lot more naturally, plus it's a whole lot more entertaining.

Remember, you're filling out these world-building details so you, the writer, can have a firm grasp of your setting—not so your reader can learn about the highly efficient plumbing system beneath the royal grounds. Like all other facets of your story, you only need to include the details that benefit the plot.

PEOPLE ARE NOT A MONOLITH

The real world does not work in absolutes. People have their own unique opinions and perspectives. While it's possible for a good chunk of your world to think a certain way or carry certain beliefs, there will inevitably be outliers.

It's normal for a country to have one system of government or a dominant religion, but it's *not* normal for every single citizen to support said government or practice said religion. Even if your government uses militant force to enforce societal norms, there will still be people who practice their beliefs in hiding and are willing to die for their cause.

So how do you know if your world-building has produced a monolith? Is there only one religion or belief system in your kingdom—or worse, the entire world? Is there only one political system, and does everyone follow it, no questions asked? Does every character have a name based on the same language or written in the same style regardless of background? These sorts of things aren't true to life. If your world-building is lacking variety, it's lacking realism.

MAGIC AND SUPERPOWERS MATTER

If a new race of magical beings suddenly appears in your world, things aren't going to continue as normal. People in the real world have strong reactions to unique clothing, let alone superpowers. If you're adding elemental magic, telekinesis, or fairies to your book, this is going to have a massive impact on the world you've created.

If this burst of magic is new, how do you think people would react? Would they be excited, curious, terrified, or all of the above? How would religious figures react? What about the government? You need to account for these responses and subsequent changes because life isn't going to continue as normal if suddenly everyone can fly.

If magic has always been a part of your setting, this is going to have a major impact on society and thus your world-building. If people have the power to control the weather, you can't write about crops dying in an unexpected drought, because farmer John would've made it rain. If disease was eradicated by a benevolent witch, that horrible illness you gave to precious little Timmy isn't going to make any sense. And if your characters can read minds, you can't rely on a deep dark secret to fuel the plot.

Think about how powers would affect day-to-day life. Consider not only the reactions people would have to these powers, but how regular folks would implement magic into their everyday activities.

AVOID WORLD-BUILDER'S DISEASE

This is for you writers who've been building your world for multiple years.

Stop.

In the writing community, we refer to this as *world-builder's disease*: when creators devote years of their life to crafting every single intricacy of a fictional land. Not only is this a waste of time, it's also a hindrance to the writing process. Quite often, those who suffer from world-builder's disease spend so much energy creating their fictional setting, only to realize they don't have a story or characters they can fit into it. They've made the world too detailed, a puzzle without any workable pieces.

While it's a good idea to have a firm grasp of your world, remember this is for *your novel*. If the details don't improve your plot, you don't need them. Keep your focus on the story itself. If years of your life have been devoted to an imaginary land, you might just be playing make-believe, or procrastinating starting your book.

Now that we have our world situated, we're moving on to outlining your book.

SUMMARY

WORLD-BUILDING

- World-building template:

- Overall setting
- World
- Continents, countries, and kingdoms
- Villages, cities, and towns
- Flora and climate
- The earth
- Animal life
- Architecture
- History
- Politics and government
- Class systems
- Racial groups
- Gender norms and expectations
- Prejudices and discrimination
- Sexual orientation
- Children
- Schooling and careers
- Societal expectations or norms
- Belief systems and customs

- Romance
- Arts
- Sports and athletics
- Clothing, accessories, or body modifications
- Ethics
- Technology, science, and magic

- Keep these tips in mind while building your world:

- *Avoid the info dump.* If the exposition doesn't move the plot forward, delete it.
- *People are not a monolith.* Not everyone in your world should look the same, have the same beliefs, or think the same way.
- *Magic and superpowers make a difference.* If magic is new to your world, how does it change society? If magic has always existed, how does it affect daily life?
- *Avoid world-builder's disease.* If you're spending years building your world, you might just be procrastinating writing your novel.

CHAPTER 6
OUTLINING YOUR BOOK

QUIT YOUR BELLYACHING, IT'S FUN!

AS MENTIONED IN CHAPTER 3, an outline is the blueprint for your book. It takes your thought dump ideas and puts them into a specific order to create some semblance of a book-shaped thing. This is going to be a guide that you will refer to constantly while writing.

There are many different kinds of outlines—certainly too many for me to list—but here are a few popular examples.

The Skeletal Outline lists the bare bones of your story beats, allowing you to fill in the gaps as you write. This is the preferred outlining method for people who like to make things up as they go but still have some direction.

The Flashlight Outline gives you a small view of the story in digestible chunks—think of the circle that the beam of a flashlight creates. This helps you focus on that section before moving on to the periphery of the beam into unknown territory.

The Topic Outline is similar to the outlines you might have written in school. You write out the events of the story in a sequential list, starting with the beginning of your novel all the way through to the end. Topic outlines typically use an alphanumeric method for organizing these points.

There are rules for writing a "proper" outline, but so long as your system works for you, it doesn't matter what your outline looks like. Some writers don't bother with technicalities and opt for a simple bullet point list. Others prefer lengthy outlines that leave no stone unturned. My outlines are usually really detailed and long—well over thirty pages —because that's what works for me. You have to figure out what works for you.

Bottom line, it doesn't matter what format you use, so long as it's easy for *you* to follow. After all, the point of an outline is to make the writing process a lot less complicated and a lot more effective.

You might be huffing and puffing at the thought of creating an outline, but I wouldn't recommend it if it wasn't incredibly beneficial to have. For starters, an outline will significantly decrease (and potentially eliminate) your chance of writer's block. You'll never be wondering what to write next, because the next scene is listed right there in your outline.

You can also say goodbye to plot holes and useless tangents, because if you've analyzed your outline, you should've been able to spot most of those issues and nip them in the bud well before you begin writing. Outlining also increases your odds of crafting a super intense climax because it allows you to plan for it ahead of time and ensure your story escalates in the juiciest way possible. Best of all, writers who outline spend significantly less time in the revising phase than writers who don't.

But Jenna, doesn't outlining ruin the creative process?

Only if you believe creating a story ruins the creative process, which makes no sense at all. Your outline is a condensed, mini version of the story. That means the act of outlining is, in itself, storytelling. This is why I have such a blast outlining my novels. I'm inventing an entire story and watching it unfold to completion.

Creating an outline is just another way to craft a story. You're still building a world, plot, conflict, and characters, but instead of writing them in lengthy, colorful sentences, you're writing them in shorthand. It's pretty amazing to see your creation mapped out in full even before you've written it.

There's a good chance you're pouting right now. Some writers are devout pantsers—writers who go in without a plan and write "by the seat of their pants." I'm not here to force your hand. You can ignore my advice completely. But if you picked up this book, there was probably a reason for it.

Is it possible to write without an outline? Yes. Is it possible you're the type of writer who doesn't need an outline? Sure. But is it also possible you don't know what the hell you're doing and need all the help you can get? Absolutely.

Like I've said, whether you outline or "pants" is ultimately up to you. But personally, I recommend making this decision based on trial and error. If you try to write without an outline only to crash and burn, take heart. If the majority of writers could create by the seat of their pants, outlines wouldn't exist in the first place. And no, contrary to what some loud (and stupid) naysayers spout, utilizing an outline doesn't make you any less of a creator.

Let's assume you've decided to give outlining a shot. Great choice! We've already covered a few options available, but quite often it helps to see someone else's system. If you need help finding your method, allow me to provide a step-by-step breakdown of my personal process. Hold the applause, my generosity requires no praise.

Gather your thought dump, character profiles, and world-building, and let's dive into the outline.

Get to the point(s)

In this first part of my outlining phase, I scan through my entire thought dump, homing in on key events and plot points: the inciting incident, first kiss, fight scenes, character deaths, the climax, and anything else that drives the plot and subplots forward. Then, I write a brief description—three to five words, max—of each point on note cards. You can use actual note cards, you can use Post-its, or you can go the digital route. If you choose the last option, I recommend a platform like Milanote, which allows you to organize various notes online, much like you would a studio wall.

Pro tip: Be sure to color code these cards. For example, I use red for violence, pink for romance, purple for friendship, etc. This makes it easier to see if you have too much or too little of certain types of content, or if you have too much of one thing in a row (like too much swapping spit for chapters upon chapters—sometimes your character needs to relax their jaw, for god's sake).

Organize

Once you have all your cards made, move to an open space. This can be a poster board, a Milanote board, or a part of the floor that *hopefully* no one will trample over. The goal is to arrange all of your plot points in the order you want them to appear in your story. I call this the puzzle phase. Each note card is its own puzzle piece, and you're trying to find the best way they fit together.

While you're doing this, you'll realize a few things. One, this is hard. Unfortunately, writing a book is hard, so consider this a glimpse into your future. Two, you're going to have big chunks of empty space in your story. This is completely normal. In fact, that's why we're doing this step in the first place. We want to find those empty spaces and figure out a way to fill them—which brings us to the next step in the puzzle phase.

Fill the holes

After you've organized everything, you're going to look for any plot holes and try to fill them. This alone could take some time because, well, plot holes are a bitch. Don't rush this process. Give yourself time to brainstorm, and by all means, utilize the help of critique partners. You may be tempted to skip this step, but trust me, you don't want to. It's a lot easier to tackle plot holes in the outlining phase versus the writing phase.

Give your readers a break

Once your holes are filled (non-sexually speaking), you should have the beginnings of an outline. It's time to divide that sucker into chapters. Find reasonable start and end points that will create natural breaks.

Pro tip: Chapters that end with a question or a surprise encourage the readers to keep turning the pages. It's also a great idea to end your chapter with a different emotion than how the chapter began.

If you're not ready for exact chapters yet, feel free to separate these plot points into days or weeks within the story.

Getting warmer

This is the part when we turn our puzzle into a full-fledged outline. If you've been using note cards or Post-its, now's the time to digitize your work; this can be via Microsoft Word, Google Docs, NovelPad, or another writing software of your choosing. If you've been using Milanote to organize your ideas, then you're a step ahead and can move on to the next point.

Get granular

Once all your plot points are in a digital document, go back to your thought dump. Are there any remaining ideas not yet reflected in your outline? If so, it's time to find their proper place.

Remember, the puzzle phase only took your main plot points into consideration. There should be a lot more details in your thought dump that haven't yet been accounted for, like streams of dialogue, physical descriptions, world-building, even fighting maneuvers. Where would they make the most sense in your outline? A physical description of your main character should be added toward the beginning of your outline, so readers know what they look like right away. Maybe you have an idea of where that one snarky conversation could take place, or when that one supporting character should kick the bucket.

Keep beefing up your outline until everything in your thought dump has found its home—except, of course, for the crap you decide not to use. Not everything in your thought dump will be worth salvaging, and that's fine. The point is to put the good stuff to use.

Review, review, review

Go through your outline and find anything that might be a problem for you later in the writing process: vague explanations, time gaps, inconsistencies, and yes, more plot holes. Save yourself some trouble in the future by adding depth to the shallow places now.

The goal is to try to make the actual writing process as seamless as possible. If you've got a scene here or there that isn't completely fleshed out, that's not a big deal. Not every moment needs to be spelled out in full. The idea is to give you a comfortable, confident image of your story.

This is also your opportunity to trim the fat from your outline. Does a character only show up in one scene? Is there any filler? Do you have scenes that read as repetitive? Delete, delete, delete. Make your outline as tight as possible so you have fewer scenes to cut during the drafting phase.

And just like that, you have an outline.

Provided you're comfortable and happy with your content, you can start writing your book. But just because you've started your book doesn't mean you can't continue to contribute to your outline.

Writer brains are wild and free. We tend to come up with ideas at random, even well after the planning phase. When this happens, pull out your outline and make the appropriate changes. Everything is modifiable. It's your outline. It's your rules.

Now that your story is mapped out, we can dive into some intricacies, starting with tense.

SUMMARY

OUTLINING YOUR BOOK

- Grab your thought dump and complete the following steps:

- Put general plot points onto physical or digital cards.
- Organize cards in order of appearance within your story.
- Find plot holes and fill them.
- Divide your outline into chapters.
- Transfer the organized cards to a digital form if you haven't already.
- Add the finer details from your thought dump into the new outline.
- Review the outline as many times as you need, looking for plot holes and inconsistencies while elaborating on content and removing filler.

CHAPTER 7

CHOOSE A TENSE
STOP TRYING TO MAKE FUTURE TENSE HAPPEN

YOU'RE ABOUT to begin the first draft of your novel, which means it's time to make a very important decision: Which tense are you going to write in? Tense refers to time; is your story happening now, or did it occur way back in yesteryear?

You need to choose a tense, and more importantly, you need to stick with it. Flip-flopping between tenses is a rookie mistake that will jar your reader so hard they might fall off their chair—or in a more realistic scenario, put your book down and never pick it up again.

The two most popular tenses you've likely read are **past** and **present**, the former reciting past events while the latter depicts actions and events unfolding—wait for it—in the present. I know, complex stuff, right?

Examining verb choice is helpful when you're exploring either of these tenses.

An example of past tense is, *She slammed her fist into the wall.*

While present tense would read, *She slams her fist into the wall.*

But Jenna! What about future tense?

How many books have you read that feature future tense? Zero? *Maybe* one? There's a reason for that. Future tense is rarely written because it's extremely difficult to utilize, and it can be especially uncomfortable to read. Simply put, it's a niche very few can master.

I know you want to be original, but you can do that via unique characters and rich worlds. You don't need an obscure tense to make your story stand out.

Which brings us back to good ole past and present tense. Choosing between the two can be tricky but understanding the pros and cons of each option can help you make an informed, reliable decision.

Past tense

One of the biggest benefits of past tense is that it's nearly invisible, as past tense is the go-to tense for most written media. Many published pieces outside of fiction, like news articles, are written in past tense. Because of this, past tense is what readers are most familiar with. Thus, they don't notice it. When you use this tense in fiction, there's no period of adjustment on the reader's part. That means they can immediately immerse themselves in the story without getting hung up on the language, which is an asset to any storyteller.

The next benefit is genre flexibility. Past tense isn't just the go-to for many forms of nonfiction, but for most genre fiction as well. Fantasy, sci-fi, and mystery novels often use past tense, so once again, readers expect it. Additionally, past tense is considered more suspenseful and believable, which are necessary traits for most stories. No matter which genre you write, there's a good chance past tense will be a natural fit for your story.

Past tense also offers writers a great deal of freedom. In theory, your story has already occurred, as it has happened in the past. This means you have the ability to hop around through time when needed. You can summarize a stuffy dinner, breeze through a boring meeting, or skip an entire season to get to the next plot point. Some writers call this fast-forwarding; you're giving the readers a peek at what happened and moving on. You can describe the moment in detail, you can use scene breaks or time skips, or you can utilize a transition. Hell, you can zip through time pretty much however you please. This freedom is specific to past tense, and it makes shifting from scene to scene significantly easier.

But no tense is perfect, and past tense has its fair share of flaws. The first is the many options: simple past, past progressive, past perfect, past perfect progressive, past insensitive, future in the past, and more. You will likely use many types of past tense throughout your writing, but if grammar isn't your forte, it may get confusing. While past tense is the more common of the two tenses, it's also considered the harder one to write, and that's largely because of all the variations you have to deal with.

The next pitfall is telling. Sure, past tense gives you the freedom to hop through time, but it also gives you the freedom to be lazy. It's a lot easier to fall into bad habits when writing in past tense, specifically the habit of telling as opposed to showing. Telling refers to merely stating actions or events within a story, whereas showing involves describing said events and creating a visceral, immersive experience—which is clearly the preferred way to go. Telling is not quite as natural in present tense, but in past tense, the door is wide open, and you have to be diligent about not walking through it.

Present tense

The clearest benefit of present tense is the immediacy it creates. Present tense illustrates actions moment by moment because the story, in theory, is happening in real time. This creates a sense of urgency. You don't necessarily need to rely on active verbs, because the tense itself is active. When used correctly, present tense can make readers feel like they're right alongside the characters experiencing the story with them.

The next benefit is casualness. There is something conversational about present tense, almost as if the story is being told by a friend rather than a formal narrator. This type of intimacy can be desirable depending on the tone and intention of your story. Often contemporary fiction is written in present tense for this very reason.

But the greatest benefit of present tense is that it's easy to write. There are only a few variations of present tense. You don't have to be grammatically inclined to get the hang of it, which is very enticing, especially if you're a novice. It's also easier to acclimate to because you're writing your protagonist's moves frame by frame. If you're looking for an easy way to get started with storytelling, present tense is a good option.

Now that present tense is looking very tempting, it's time to drop a turd in the punch bowl. What's present tense's greatest pitfall? It can be awkward. Since past tense is the standard for most written work, present tense tends to stand out in a big way. That means for most genres, if you're writing in present tense, the readers are going to notice and probably be a little jarred.

If present tense is your final choice, readers will just have to adjust—but if you're a shitty writer, that adjustment might never come. People who are used to past tense often feel that present tense comes off as a sporting event play-by-play. It may be easier to make mistakes with past tense, but it's also easier to get readers comfortable with the story. Present tense doesn't have that benefit.

The last pitfall is that it's inflexible with time. You don't get to breeze past boring moments like in the past tense, because you're stuck in the now. This can make things difficult because not every moment of your character's life is going to be riveting. You don't want to write about your character picking their nose or taking a whiz, do you? In this case, your options are mostly limited to time skips, but even then, too many scene breaks in rapid succession can make your story feel choppy. This puts writers into a bit of a pickle.

Comparing the two tenses side-by-side, the breakdown is clear: Present tense is easier to write, and past tense is easier to read. But you can make either tense work in your favor. Ultimately, your job is to choose the tense that fits your story best. Hone your craft and get feedback so you can make whichever tense you choose a wonderful fit.

Now that you have your tense locked in, let's look at point of view.

SUMMARY

CHOOSE A TENSE

- Review the pros and cons of past and present tense, and stick with one throughout your story.

- Past tense:

  - Pro: It's invisible, because ninety percent of media uses it.
  - Pro: It's genre flexible, as it's the chosen tense of most genre fiction.
  - Pro: It gives you freedom to transition your characters through the story, as the events have already happened.
  - Con: There are so many options! Brush up on your grammar skills before choosing this tense.
  - Con: It's easier to "tell" with stories in the past tense; don't fall for that bad habit.

- Present tense:

  - Pro: The story reads as immediate, giving you an automatic sense of urgency.
  - Pro: It's naturally casual, allowing your reader to stay close to the story.

- Pro: It's easier to write for a novice author.
- Con: It's awkward to read, as most media is written in past tense.
- Con: It's inflexible, as you can't breeze through transitions in time. Utilize scene breaks to avoid this issue.

CHAPTER 8
POINTS OF VIEW
BECAUSE PERSPECTIVE MATTERS

THE POINT of view of your book is the lens through which your readers are experiencing the story. As mentioned in Chapter 3, the most popular points of view are first person and third person.

First person tells the story from the character's point of view. For example, *I slammed the door*.

Third person tells the story through an outside narrator's perspective. For example, *She/He/They slammed the door*.

As for the ever-elusive second person point of view, we don't know her.

Second person point of view tells the story from your perspective. For example, *You slammed the door*. Like future tense, it's very seldom used, and there's a reason for that. It's awkward and ill-fitting for most plotlines, except for choose-your-own-adventure stories.

What I'm trying to say is, don't screw up your novel for the sake of being "not like other writers." Stick with the points of view that work best. And if you're not quite sure if first person or third person is right for you, allow me to make the decision a whole lot easier.

First person

As we covered, first person is when a character of the novel, usually the main character, is also the narrator. The perspective of the story is told using the pronouns "I" or "we." It's also possible for there to be more than one first person perspective in a novel. Maybe two characters are narrating every other chapter within the book. This is perfectly fine as long as you make a clear distinction between which chapter or section is being narrated by which character.

Similar to present tense, one of the benefits of first person point of view is the casualness. Your character is telling their story to the reader, which gives it an informal, almost conversational feel. If this is what you're going for, then first person is the perfect choice. This point of view is often regarded as intimate, due to the close bond created between the main character and the reader.

Another benefit of first person is ease. Many people consider this point of view the easiest perspective to write in. After all, you're using the pronouns "I" and "we," which makes it much easier for you to put yourself in the character's position. If you're looking to make the writing process as effortless as possible, first person is a smart way to go.

Next, we look at voice. If characterization is your strong suit, writing in first person is going to be especially enjoyable. This point of view allows you to breathe life and authenticity into whichever character is narrating your novel. And if you're skilled at characterization, that means readers are probably going to love your narrator.

Which brings us to the downsides of first person point of view, starting with voice.

But Jenna, you said this was a benefit!

It certainly is—if you're great at characterization. Through first person point of view, your story is being told by a character, which means their voice has to be impeccable. You can't slip in and out between your personal voice and their voice. They are the narrator, not you. If you're not skilled at carrying that voice, the narration is either going to be inconsistent or flat.

Even worse, if you've created an unlikeable character with an irritating voice, you've got a big problem. The readers are experiencing the entire story through that voice—and if the voice is shitty? Yikes. They'll put the book down fast.

The final, and possibly greatest, downside is limitation. You're stuck in the mind of this character. You don't get to narrate anything that's happening beyond their frame of reference. If something goes down at the villain's headquarters, readers aren't going to see it. That may not be a problem given the nature of your story, but this completely ruins the concept for some writers, resulting in an entire rewrite—or simply a new point of view.

Which brings us to our second option.

Third person

Third person point of view utilizes an outside narrator who isn't part of the cast of characters. The pronouns used throughout the story are "he," "she," or "they." The narrator is either all-knowing, following the entire cast and every move made, or they stick to following a particular character, their moves, and their decisions. If you're choosing the last option, it's perfectly fine to follow more than one character. However, just like with first person point of view, you need to make a clear distinction between which character the narrator is following by separating the perspectives in different scenes or chapters.

The most obvious benefit to third person is variety. Unlike with first person point of view, third person offers a ton of perspectives to choose from. A few of the more popular ones are:

Third person omniscient, which assumes an all-knowing perspective. Think of the narrator as an omnipotent god.

Third person limited, which restricts the narrator to following only one character's actions and perspective. Think of the narrator as a shadow hanging over the character's shoulder.

Then there's **third person deep**, where the narrator is restricted to one character, but this perspective takes a deeper dive into the character's mental and emotional state. Think of the narrator as a demon living in the character's brain.

With so many options, you're bound to find a perspective that works for your story. Want to write about anything and everything, no matter the characters involved? Try third person omniscient. Want the reader to develop a close, intimate relationship with one character? Third person deep is perfect for you.

Similar to first person, another benefit of third person point of view is voice. If you're comfortable with your personal narrative style, then third person is going to be a breeze. You don't have to worry about sticking to one character's voice throughout the entire novel, because you get to write in your own voice, your own preference, your own style.

The last benefit is formality. While first person has a more casual feel, third person is the opposite. There's a refinement to third person, since the story is being told by a nameless, faceless, and sometimes all-knowing narrator. If that's what you're going for, then third person is the obvious choice. It sets a very clear tone and intention.

But no point of view is perfect, and third person isn't any different. The biggest issue writers run into is causing confusion. Remember all those different third person points of view you have to choose from? Well, sometimes it can be hard to distinguish one from the other. Maybe you've chosen third person deep, and then suddenly you find yourself narrating the thoughts and feelings of *other* characters. This is often referred to as head hopping, and it can be jarring for readers. There's also the issue of overusing the "he," "she," and "they" pronouns, which can leave readers disoriented; which "he" are we talking about? The main character, his brother, or his best friend? They're all in the same scene!

Basically, when writing in third person point of view, you have to make sure both you and the reader are clear on the perspective being followed.

The final pitfall is specific to third person omniscient: distance. With third person omniscient, an outside narrator is recounting the events as opposed to a character themselves or a narrator closely linked to a character. This can create a divide between the reader and the cast, which may make them less invested in the story. This is largely why third person omniscient has a reputation for being stuffy or boring; readers are less connected to the characters, which can break the immersion.

If you're adamant about using third person but still want to create an emotional bond between the reader and character, consider third person deep instead.

So, which point of view should you choose?

You're going to get tired of me saying this, but it really depends on what works best for your story. Forget finding the flawless option because there is none. Ultimately, you have to choose whatever fits your plot, intention, and tone. You can experiment with different points of view to see which works best, or you can simply rely on your gut instinct. Certain stories are naturally better suited for specific points of view.

With all your details in place and your outline on standby, we're finally ready to draft this masterpiece!

SUMMARY

POINTS OF VIEW

- Review the pros and cons of both first and third person, and choose which is best for your story.

- First person: This is the perspective from a specific character's point of view. Most of the time, the pronouns "I" and "we" are used.

- Pro: The book reads as casual, since your character is telling the story to the reader with an almost conversational tone.
- Pro: Using the pronouns "I" and "we" makes it much easier for you to put yourself in the character's position.
- Pro: If characterization is your strong suit, first person allows you to breathe life and authenticity into whichever character is narrating your novel.
- Con: The story is being told by a character, which means you must have their voice down. Unfortunately, if that voice is unlikeable or irritating, your readers aren't going to enjoy it.
- Con: You're stuck in the mind of this character, so you don't get to narrate anything happening beyond their frame of reference.

- Third person: This point of view uses a narrator outside the story's events. The pronouns "she," "he," and "they" are used.

- Pro: You have many third person points of view to choose from, such as third person omniscient, third person limited, and third person deep.
- Pro: If you're comfortable in your personal narrative style, third person allows you to write in your own voice.
- Pro: Third person feels serious and refined.
- Con: Sometimes writers confuse the different third person types and start blending them. This confusion often transfers over to the reader.
- Con: Third person omniscient can create a divide between the reader and the cast, which may make readers less invested in the story.

- How do you choose which one to use?

- Experiment with different points of view to see what works best.
- Use your gut instinct. Certain stories are naturally better suited for specific points of view.

CHAPTER 9
WRITING THE FIRST DRAFT

DEEP BREATHS . . .

THE FIRST DRAFT, also known as the rough draft, is the first written version of your story. A lot of people struggle with writing the first draft, so much so that most never make it past this step.

While this is disheartening, it's not particularly surprising. First drafts are a monumental undertaking that can leave people feeling completely out of their depth.

Fortunately, it doesn't have to be that big of a deal. Any multi-published author can tell you that getting over the hump and establishing a routine makes the drafting process so much easier to navigate. Luckily, you have a multi-published author at your disposal ready to bestow her wisdom.

It's me. I'm the author.

Let's make that first draft as smooth as possible—and a whole lot less scary.

Accept the suckage

The first draft is a shitshow. You'll inevitably have moments when you're typing across your keyboard and all that's appearing on the page is pure crap.

It's exceedingly rare for your writing to come out perfect the first time around. You'll be tempted to type and delete and type and delete ad nauseam.

Don't do it.

Get this through your head right now: *Your first draft is going to suck.* This is a reality of the writing process. No one finishes this draft with their dignity intact.

Believe it or not, this is not my way of discouraging you. Accepting the suckage makes the first draft much easier to plow through. The reason so many writers fail to make it past draft one is because they're demoralized by their less-than-perfect writing. Aren't I supposed to be a creative genius? What's all this nonsense spewed across the page?

I'm willing to bet no one told you creative genius takes drafts upon drafts to concoct. Remember, it's called a *rough* draft for a reason. If you allow yourself to dish out some shitty writing, you just might finish this first draft. And guess what happens after that?

You get to take all that suckage and turn it into art.

But that's a problem for another day. Right now, focus on getting words on the page, however terrible they may be. You can improve them during the next draft, but you can't revise a blank page.

Set goals

Goal setting is an asset to writers, particularly during the first draft. There are two types of goal setting methods writers can explore: long-term and short-term goals.

Let's start with long-term goals. Some writers opt to set yearly goals, but I strongly discourage this. Remember those new year's resolutions you set? Yeah, me neither. That's the thing about giving yourself a year to achieve a goal; it's easy to forget about it a few weeks later.

Instead, consider using the quarterly method for your long-term goals. This gives you three months—roughly ninety days—to complete a particular writing task. During the drafting phase, my typical quarterly goal is to write one hundred pages, but you need to create a goal that works for you and your schedule.

What's great about the quarterly goal method is it has Goldilocks syndrome. The amount of time is not too long, not too short, but just right. If you give yourself six months to a year to complete a goal, it's easy to procrastinate or forget entirely. If you give yourself one month to complete a goal, that's a lot of pressure, and you may freeze up or panic. But three months allows you just enough give and take to light a fire under your ass without immobilizing you.

But when it comes to creating writing habits, particularly during the first draft, it's especially important to set short-term goals.

Short-term goals are typically made on a daily-to-weekly basis. In these situations, we're strictly looking at productivity, which can be achieved in a variety of ways.

First, we've got **word count goals**, where you're holding yourself to getting a certain number of words on the page by the end of the day or the week. Next are **page count goals**, where you're trying to write a certain number of pages in a set amount of time. Lastly, there are **scene goals**, where you're trying to reach or complete a scene. For example, your goal may be to tackle a tricky fight scene, or you want to finish writing the chapter by the end of the day.

Feel free to experiment with different short-term goals until you find a method that suits your process best. Scene goals work best for me, whereas some writers swear by word count goals.

The point is, you have to set some kind of goal in order to hold yourself accountable. These smaller goals add up quickly, helping you to achieve your long-term goals and ultimately finish your first draft.

Prioritize habit over motivation

Motivation is fantastic, but it comes and goes. Instead of waiting around for motivation to strike, focus on forming habits—a writing routine you hold yourself to.

Writing your first draft isn't all excitement and inspiration. You will inevitably have hard scenes and slow slogs, and in those instances, motivation will be a distant memory. Creating a habit is pivotal if you want to get through the tough days. This doesn't mean you have to write every day; many people can't due to their obligations or lifestyle. But this does mean you have to create a system that works for you and your schedule. This could mean writing three days a week, writing for an hour each day after work, or devoting every weekend to your manuscript. Whatever you choose, stick to it.

The first week will probably be the easiest, because you're energized and proactive. After that, this whole habit thing is going to get rough. That's when you really need to push yourself. Fight through the lack of motivation, and remind yourself why you're doing this. You're creating a fabulous book baby!

After about a month of grueling labor, your new writing schedule will feel natural, almost instinctive, and that's when you know the habit has formed. Once you reach this stage, your writing will be a lot more consistent, which means your first draft will get written a lot quicker.

Don't read it

I know it's tempting, but trust me on this. Don't read your story while you're writing it. This is how people get stuck in an endless loop of editing. They read what they've written, hate it, rewrite it, still hate it, rewrite it, and so on, until they're crying in the fetal position clutching a bottle of chianti.

Can you tell I've had personal experience with this?

This is a problem for countless writers. They pump out words, read what they've written, realize it's a clusterfuck, and pound that delete button. The obvious way to eliminate this issue is to *not read what you're writing*. That's not to say you should never read your first draft, but for the love of god, don't read it in the middle of a writing session. Get those words on the page, however sucky they may be, and save the reading for another day.

I promise, if you allow yourself to sleep on it, that messy first draft will look a lot less ominous upon reading.

Don't edit it . . . unless you have to

Speaking of an endless editing loop, that's the quickest way to never finish your first draft. After all, you can't finish a draft if you're constantly rewriting it.

That is why so many writers swear by one sacred first draft rule: *Don't edit as you go.* Save that for the second draft. If the idea of perfecting your writing sends you spiraling, then this is a rule you ought to heed.

But sometimes rules are made to be broken. There is a minority of writers who have the opposite problem; they can't move forward without mid-draft edits, because their mind is fixated on all the changes left to be made. This immobilizes them, which leaves their writing at a standstill. If you're one of these few writers, then it's okay to edit as you go—within reason. I suggest making quick, easy edits, and saving the larger ones for the second draft. Leave notes in the margin or color code problem areas so you can easily address them in the future.

Find your drafting rhythm

Similar to making your own habits, finding a rhythm requires trial and error. Throughout this process, you'll notice certain methods that work for you versus those that fall flat.

Some writers swear by word count goals, whereas those only encourage me to word vomit filler onto the page. Some writers need pure silence, whereas others write with music playing in the background. I have friends who love writing sprints—a method involving setting a timer for fifteen minutes and writing like the wind—whereas other writers find sprinting to be an unnecessary pressure.

Where do you fall within this spectrum? Give a few options a try and see what sticks.

For inspiration, how about I share my personal drafting method. I'm one of the few folks who needs to edit as they go, so you'll see that accounted for in my routine.

First, I will spend a day writing, plowing through my draft without reading anything I've written. I usually give myself a scene goal, and I aim to complete said scene by the time my writing session is over.

The next day, I read everything I wrote during the previous session. This gives me enough distance from the session that I'm able to look at my work through a more objective lens. While reading, I make quick, easy edits, like deleting filler or tweaking dialogue. Any time-consuming edits get color coded so I can sort them out later.

Once I've finished my brief edit, I continue writing the story where I left off, and the cycle repeats itself the next day.

Will this method work for you? Who knows? Don't feel the need to emulate it. Just remember writing takes practice, and it's up to you to create a routine that suits you best.

Create a list

As you draft, you'll start to notice your weaknesses. Maybe you abuse the hell out of filter words (We'll cover those in Chapter 21). Maybe your descriptions are lacking, or maybe you genuinely have no idea how commas work.

Don't ignore these issues. This is a fantastic learning opportunity. Capitalize on it.

If you're the type who edits as you go, then you can potentially tackle your weaknesses in the first draft. You can also plug your writing into a grammar checker and have it point out your issues. I personally prefer ProWritingAid, as it not only highlights your mistakes but teaches you how to avoid them in the future.

If you're not comfortable editing as you go—which, as we covered, is the majority mindset—jot down a list of your problem areas. By the time you finish your first draft, you should have an easy reference guide of everything you need to tackle in draft two.

It's not done

A lot of writers finish the first draft only to lament that it's a steaming pile of shit.

Remember what I said about the rough draft? It's *rough*. But for a lot of writers, that reality doesn't truly set in until draft one is complete. They whine and complain about how imperfect it is. Even if they edited it along the way, the story is nowhere near what they wanted it to be.

That's because it's not done yet.

Of course your story sucks. It's *incomplete*. The first draft exists to lay the groundwork, not to erect the entire building. This is just phase one of a much larger, grander picture. You have ten or more drafts to write and multiple rounds of self-editing, not to mention at least three varieties of professional editing, several phases of proofreading—and don't get me started on the publishing steps.

You see? There's no need to fret. Take some calming breaths and relax. Your first draft may be done, but that's just the start of it. You have plenty of time to make this book into the work of art it's destined to become. The fact that you've finished this draft in the first place warrants a major pat on the back.

And a cocktail if you're legal and so inclined.

Bottom line, if the first draft isn't the story you imagined, it's no big deal. You can improve it in round two, starting with the first chapter.

SUMMARY
WRITING THE FIRST DRAFT

- Following these tips will help get you through the first draft of your novel:

- Your first draft is going to suck. Accept that.
- Set long-term and short-term goals to hold yourself accountable.
- Be consistent by creating writing habits.
- Don't read the manuscript while writing. Focus on getting words on the page during your writing session.
- Don't edit the book while writing, unless you have to. If you do revise as you write, make sure the edits are quick. Keep moving forward!
- Find your drafting rhythm by trying different techniques and methods and sticking to the ones that work best for you.
- Create a list of your weaknesses to further improve your drafting skills.
- Remember, your first draft is not the end! It's okay if it's imperfect because you have time to fix any mistakes.

CHAPTER 10
WRITING THE FIRST CHAPTER

IT'S THE HARDEST ONE. SORRY.

LET'S FACE IT: The first chapter can be a real kick in the dick. Hell, there are workshops dedicated to writing the perfect *first page*. That's a lot of pressure straight out the gate, and it can be enough to crush a writer.

The first chapter is a scary undertaking because it's the beginning of your entire book. You have to hook the reader right then and there, and if you don't, they may not stick around for more. It sucks, but it's important. That's why I'm giving you the dos and don'ts of getting your first chapter on the right track.

Do: Start the story with a bang

How many books have you read that open with a description of the weather or the history of a kingdom? Starting with a bang may seem obvious, but it's often overlooked.

The goal is simple. Your opening scene should be entertaining, engaging, and most importantly, an appropriate reflection of the overall story. That means if your book is an explosive adventure, the opening scene should be action-packed. If the book is a comedy, the opening scene should tickle your reader's funny bone.

This needs to happen from the start so readers know exactly what they're in for. You don't want them waiting chapters upon chapters for the actual story to occur.

Sometimes writers struggle to bring the action this early on. After all, isn't that what the inciting incident is for? But there are plenty of ways to give readers a taste of what's to come without skipping important structural steps. For example, it's common for romance novels to begin with a dramatic breakup or a dating fail. This showcases the main character's singleness while letting readers know to expect romantic shenanigans. Because *The Savior's Champion* opens with the gruesome murder of a queen, the readers know from the start to expect bloodshed.

Now keep in mind, your goal is to hook readers with the first chapter—not necessarily the first sentence. One of the most common pieces of writing advice floating around is that the first sentence is most important. If the reader isn't hooked from the first sentence, they won't read the rest of the book, right?

This rule exists mostly for the querying process. Agents get a lot of manuscripts to flip through, so if you're going the traditional publishing route, you'll want to make sure your first sentence is powerful enough to catch their attention. Of course, regardless of your publishing route, you want your first sentence to be stellar. But you can achieve this with one clause—or hell, one *word*.

Herein lies the issue: The pressure to create the perfect opening line often leads to a rambling, ridiculous sentence that turns the readers off. Don't try to fit an essay into your first sentence. Yes, your opener needs to be strong, but it doesn't need to be lengthy to make an impact. Focus instead on making that first *scene* a heavy hitter.

Don't: Info dump the world

I'm looking at you, fantasy and sci-fi authors. The first chapter should not be a history lesson of how the galaxy formed, or a timeline of the realm's royal dynasty. You want to set the scene and allow readers to feel transported into the world, but not at the expense of the story. Beginning with an info dump is the exact opposite of opening with a bang, and I'm willing to wager 75 percent of the information you presented isn't relevant to the story.

You may be pointing to classic pieces of literature as a defense, but literature evolves over time. People expect the classics to be written as . . . well, classics. But when they pick up a piece of modern literature, they're expecting a completely different voice—one that gets to the fucking point.

Rather than burdening your reader with useless factoids, explain those bits and pieces of the world as they become relevant. When the characters are navigating difficult terrain, address the climate. When they visit the castle, divulge about the monarchy. And yes, a little exposition is sometimes necessary, but limit it to the essentials. If you've written more than a page of exposition, you've gone too far.

Remember, this is the first chapter of your book. A history lesson may be interesting to you, but that's because you're already emotionally invested. Your readers haven't even met the main character, let alone created an attachment. Focus on captivating the reader and creating that immersion, and unveil the world naturally as the story develops.

Do: Begin where the story begins

This tip is closely linked to the previous one. Many writers make the mistake of including a ton of backstory at the start of a novel. Before you write it, ask yourself, does this directly influence my story? Does my plot fail without this content? If the answer is no, I promise you, your readers don't care about it.

Begin where the story begins. If you're not sure how to do that, refer to Chapter 2 and brush up on structure. Most stories start with a look at the main character's normal life, along with an introduction to their desires or dilemma. Simply put, you are showing the reader how the character is living and why it's not ideal for them. Something is going wrong in the main character's life, and they're either ignoring it, struggling to handle it, or desperate to fix it.

This is vital for the opening chapter because it establishes two things: the conflict of the story as well as the main character's goals. These two elements directly lead into your inciting incident, which is the moment when your main character embarks on their journey, either through personal choice or because they're forced into action. And that's another reason why you must establish these details early on, as the inciting incident typically occurs within the first two or three chapters.

Don't: Stay in in the normal world forever

There's nothing exciting about normalcy. Give us a glimpse of it and move on.

This is where a lot of writers get hung up. They'll start their book with chapters upon chapters of the main character going to school, going to work, going to the market—you know, the boring shit. You can give the reader an idea of this person's life without taking them through every tedious minute of it.

Instead of having the character wake up, brush their teeth, and sit through an entire day of school, start the chapter at the end of their final class while they're staring at the clock and waiting for the bell to ring. This lets the reader know how mind-numbingly dull their life is without making your audience want to end it all with them.

You only need a snapshot, something that juxtaposes the turbulence of the plot. Establishing normalcy should take less than a chapter. After that, move on to something interesting.

Do: Introduce your main character

Your first chapter absolutely must follow at least one of your protagonists. If there are any exceptions to this rule, I'm failing to think of them.

You may want your book to open with the villain's perspective, or the perspective of a character who was alive well before your protagonist was even born. That sounds like the ideal set up for a prologue, but probably not the first chapter.

The goal of your first chapter is to hook readers, and assuming you succeed at this, they will become invested in whichever character is leading the way. What a shame it would be if the main perspective of the chapter isn't the protagonist's—and how annoying for your reader! Can you imagine becoming totally immersed in a voice only for it to never appear again? Talk about a bait and switch.

Don't: Panic

Don't waste time trying to perfect the first draft of your first chapter, because it's a losing battle. Instead, move on with your story. Allow that steaming pile to stink for a while. You can hose it down later.

Remember, obsessing over perfection is the biggest issue writers have with their first draft. If you obsess over making the first chapter flawless, you'll never finish your book.

Yes, there is a lot of pressure to make this chapter amazing, but you're not doing yourself any favors by succumbing to the stress. The truth is, you're not yet capable of writing a wonderful first chapter. This is true for all writers. We improve as we write, which means the writer you are tomorrow will be better than the writer you are today. Once you go back to edit your first chapter, you'll be doing so as a stronger, more competent creator. Let *that* person perfect the first chapter. I'm more than confident they'll get the job done.

On top of that, you won't be alone in this process. You are going to have multiple rounds of beta readers, critique partners, editors, and proofreaders. There will be lots of time and help to make this chapter shine. So relax. Even if you're not capable of writing a great chapter now, you will be when the time comes to edit.

What's the bottom line?

The first chapter of your novel is designed to make your readers care. This is accomplished when you combine all of the previous notes— opening with a bang, following the main character, and introducing their problems and goals. Readers won't get emotionally invested if you're waxing poetic about your kingdom's irrigation system, or if the main character's life is fine and dandy, and they certainly won't get invested if you're not following the main character at all. This three-part punch of engagement, perspective, and dilemma is designed to evoke your reader's empathy.

Use your opening chapter to showcase your main character's humanity. What makes them relatable? What makes them likeable? What are their goals, and why should the readers care about their problems? Vulnerability in the first chapter is key to getting your readers invested. Lean into that feeling, and let it work to your advantage.

With the first chapter safely tucked away, let's discuss how to perfect every other chapter from this point forward.

SUMMARY

WRITING THE FIRST CHAPTER

- Keep the dos and don'ts in mind when writing your first chapter.

- Do:

  - Start the story with a bang. Open your book with an interesting scene that carries impact while mirroring the overall tone of your story.
  - Begin where the story begins, keeping the details relevant to what the reader needs to know.
  - Introduce your main character and their problem. Show the main character's humanity and relatability.

- Don't:

  - Info dump. Instead, build the world as the story progresses, not all at once at the start of the first chapter.
  - Stay in the main character's normal life forever, because that's boring for the reader.
  - Panic over perfecting the rough draft of the first chapter. You will grow as a writer by finishing the first draft of the book. Afterward, you can go back with your new wisdom and tweak the first chapter to your heart's desire.

CHAPTER 11
A CHAPTER ABOUT CHAPTERS
SO META

BOOKS ARE TYPICALLY DIVIDED up into smaller digestible parts, and these parts are called chapters. They're usually numbered, though some authors (like yours truly) also give each chapter a title, which is fun but unnecessary. Chapters allow your reader to find natural pauses within the story; this helps with the flow of your plot as well as making the content feel less overwhelming. It also gives your reader the opportunity to take a break from reading, but only if they must. If you're doing your job correctly, they shouldn't want to put your book down.

What's the point of a chapter?

The goal of each chapter is to move the plot forward, which means every single chapter must showcase at least one major plot point. It's also common for subplots to be featured alongside the main plot, so if your chapter moves any subplots forward, that's great too.

But Jenna, my chapter doesn't have any plot points, but it's great for character development. That's okay, right?

Wrong.

In situations such as these, "character development" is simply a synonym for filler—content that adds no value to the story. Of course, character development is important to any novel, but your character should be able to develop through the plot and subplots, making any filler, as its name suggests, unnecessary.

If your main plot is a fantastic adventure, you should have plenty of plot-centric moments to showcase your character's fear, strength, or curiosity. If you're featuring a romantic subplot, then you'll have lots of opportunities to show off your character's flirtatious side or their blossoming sexuality.

Simply put, you don't need to include an entire chapter that's strictly fleshing out the main character. Not only will this bore the reader and disrupt the flow of your story, but it also doesn't make sense. You should already be developing your character through your plot points.

Not sure if your chapter is filler? Imagine it's removed from the novel. Can the plot move forward despite its absence? If yes, then you've got a whole lot of words to delete.

When should I create chapters?

As I mentioned in Chapter 6, the outlining phase is the ideal time to divide your story into chapters. Look for natural breaks between scenes that could easily translate into a segue from one chapter to the next. Maybe the next scene is the start of a new day, or maybe a scene ends with the perfect cliffhanger. These stopping points are way more obvious while outlining versus when writing the story itself.

Furthermore, each chapter has its own structure, featuring a beginning, middle, and an end. Because of this, it's extremely problematic—and honestly stupid—to write your novel straight through only to divide it into chapters after the fact. This will require significant restructuring and setting the scene of each chapter, including introductions, transitions, and proper endings. Sounds like a headache, right? You can avoid that mess by planning your chapters ahead of time.

The Roller-Coaster Method

How should you start and end chapters? The logical answer is to look for natural breaks in the story, but there's a trick to starting and ending chapters in a way that will effectively hook the reader. I like to call it the Roller-Coaster Method.

No matter which genre you're writing, you want your reader emotionally invested in your story. The chapter may be over, but you're hoping they'll turn the page anyway. So, what makes readers put a book down? Usually, it's because the book is dull, it's predictable, it isn't catching the reader's attention, or it's exhausting to get through.

Sounds like an easy fix. Just add some excitement, right? But that's not necessarily the case. Sure, a fight scene is exciting, but after reading three back-to-back slaughter fests, the fun is going to fizzle out. No one's on the edge of their seat anymore. Due to the immediate repetition of the same type of scene, you've managed to make gaping wounds and severed limbs boring.

The key to keeping your reader engaged isn't necessarily to make the story itself unpredictable, but to make the *emotional tone* unpredictable. The mood and momentum must constantly change, taking your reader from a fast scene to a slow scene, a soft moment to intense drama. The easiest way to do this is to employ the Roller-Coaster Method—starting and ending each chapter with a different emotion. If a chapter opens with humor, it should end with an entirely different feeling, like lust or terror. If a chapter opens with action, it could end with calm, rest, or peace. This method is flexible and has one simple objective: Make sure your reader is feeling something different by the end of the chapter.

This works for any genre no matter the stakes or intensity. Writing a fluffy romance? No problem. You can start a chapter with a swoon-worthy date, and end it with a dreaded run-in with the ex. Just like that, we've moved from heart flutters to humiliation. You've stayed true to the tone of your story without making it stagnant or stale.

Pro tip: Cliffhangers are your friend. Utilize them! They're a great tool for keeping your reader guessing, and an even better tool for getting them to turn the page. Coupling a cliffhanger with the Roller-Coaster Method will give you that coveted "unputdownable" tag that authors absolutely crave for their reviews.

Does size really matter?

When it comes to chapter length, there's no fixed rule. They are however long they need to be to tell whichever part of the story you're trying to tell. Sometimes chapters are long. Sometimes they're short. I've read chapters that were three pages and others that were thirty. As the ancient proverb goes, it's not the size of the chapter that matters, but what you do with it. So long as it's well-written, entertaining, and vital to moving the plot forward, you've done your job. There's no need to add filler chapters to meet some imagined norm or delete imperative chapters because your book is getting hefty. Who doesn't love a big burly book?

And since we're talking about length, no, your chapters don't need to be the same length. How would that even be possible? I'm a perfectionist, and even I couldn't manage to create matchy-matchy chapters. Focus on telling your story in the most entertaining and efficient way possible. Readers don't make it a habit of counting chapter page lengths and comparing the figures. They're too busy, you know, *reading*.

Creating intrigue

You've ditched the filler, you're strapped into the roller coaster, and you've stopped stressing over page count. These are all great moves, but there's one last tip to perfecting each chapter of your novel, and it's cemented in intrigue.

Sure, emotional highs and lows add intensity, but rousing curiosity and fascination is another beast entirely. This comes down to how much information you reveal versus what you save for later. A great chapter will answer enough questions to move the plot forward while creating even more questions to keep people reading.

That is why cliffhangers are so effective. Readers are left wondering, *Is he going to make it? Will she get the job?* But you don't need a cliffhanger to answer or create questions. The plot points featured in each chapter should do the job just fine.

Say you reveal a shocking plot twist: The protagonist's father did not, in fact, kill her mother. Just like that, you've both answered a question and created one. You've revealed the father's innocence while leaving readers to wonder who the real killer is.

If you're not sure if your chapters are strong enough, examine the intrigue level. Each chapter should provide closure to previous events while opening new cans of worms to wriggle around the page. Your reader should never end a chapter feeling like all their questions were answered, because then there's no need to continue reading.

Now that your chapters are shaping up beautifully, it's time to examine your story on a scene-by-scene basis.

SUMMARY

A CHAPTER ABOUT CHAPTERS

- Books are typically divided into smaller, digestible parts called chapters.

- Chapters are important because they move the plot forward. Each chapter must showcase at least one main plot point (and sometimes a subplot too).

- Filler chapters feature no main plot points and should be removed from the story.

- The outlining phase is the ideal time to divide your story into chapters because it's easier to find natural pauses within the plot.

- Hook the reader in unpredictable ways by using the Roller-Coaster Method: changing the mood and momentum of the start of the chapters versus their endings—or adding a cliffhanger.

- Chapters are as long as they need to be and can vary in length. If they are well-written, entertaining, and relevant to the story, size doesn't matter.

- A great chapter will provide enough answers to move the plot forward while still creating more questions to keep people reading.

CHAPTER 12

SETTING THE SCENE
WITHOUT BORING YOUR READERS TO TEARS

EVERY FICTION BOOK is broken down into chapters, and each chapter is broken down into smaller scenes. Scenes can be mini stories in themselves, so it's important to ground your reader in the moment, giving them a proper sense of where they are and what to expect.

Writers do this by setting the scene.

In order to set the scene, you need to establish three things up front: the character's perspective, the when and where of the moment, and the intention of the scene.

CHARACTER'S PERSPECTIVE

Readers need to know which character they're following in any given scene. Establishing this is easy. All you have to do is use their name.

Yup, just like that.

Of course, if you're writing in first person point of view, you'll most likely be using the pronouns "I" and "me." If you're only following one character throughout the entire book, then this shouldn't be an issue; readers will know the "I" in question is the same character they followed in the last chapter and the chapter before that.

If you're writing from multiple perspectives, it's helpful to list the new perspective as a chapter heading. You can do this for third person perspective novels as well. In the third book of my series, *The Savior's Army*, Chapter 1 follows Tobias, whereas Chapter 2 follows Leila. While chapter headings aren't necessarily a part of the scene, they can assist you in dictating perspective if you're writing multiple points of view.

Aside from simply labeling the perspective, you want the character to feel as real as if they were physically present in that moment. This will make the experience visceral for the reader and help them imagine they're traveling alongside the character.

I have two handy tips for grounding a character within a scene.

Use your five senses

When you write, it helps to get inside your body. Think about how you would physically feel or react to a particular situation. The perfect example of this is utilizing your five senses while setting the scene. This will not only help describe the setting, but it'll also allow your readers to feel what your character is feeling.

Let's start with the easiest sense to write: **sight**. What is the character seeing? This is where you describe the look of the space around them, which we'll elaborate on later.

Next is **smell**. A lot of writers neglect this sense, but smells can be extremely transportive. Scent creates an instant reaction. A smell can be sexy, like cologne. It can make you feel good, like chocolate chip cookies. And of course, a stench can be revolting, like body odor or piss. Choosing the proper scent can go a long way in creating a very clear picture of the scene.

Taste is another neglected sense, because unless a character is eating, we don't usually consider it. But what if the character has just gotten into a fight and can still taste blood on their lips? Has an odor ever been so pungent, you could taste its bitterness? Both these examples create an instant tone in very few words.

Touch is one of the most important senses because people have very strong reactions to it. Touch creates pleasure, pain, comfort, and fear. Is your character waking up in the warm embrace of their lover, or does the scene open with heavy shackles weighing down their wrists? These are two very different types of touch that immediately ground the reader.

And lastly, **sound** can create drastically different tones when combined with other senses. The rustling of leaves could be a calming sound if there's a warm breeze on a sunny day. On the other hand, it can be horrifying if it's the dead of night, and your character is hiding in the woods from a killer.

You don't have to use every sense. If your character doesn't taste anything, leave it alone. Nothing particularly interesting to smell? Then keep it moving. But conveying the appropriate senses will have a profound impact on your reader's immersion in the story.

Establish a tone or energy

Think about how your character is feeling, or how you want your reader feeling during each scene. If your character is depressed, then the tone of the scene should be depressing. That means no warm fuzzy descriptors like the soft touch of a silk blanket or the soothing scent of lavender. Think about descriptors that feel sad or empty, like stale air and dim lighting.

If your character is depressed in a beautiful, well-lit, colorful location, don't set the scene as it is. Instead, describe the setting through the lens of the depressed character. Maybe the colors are blurred, the laughter is muted, and the hugs are barely discernable against their flesh. This allows the readers to understand that, while the setting may be joyous, the main character isn't able to connect with it due to their state of mind.

Remember, the readers are experiencing the story through this character. That means their interpretation matters significantly, and you want to set the tone based on their view.

WHEN AND WHERE

This step involves setting the physical scene. You're describing the time and location to avoid confusing your reader. If it's Tuesday and your character is in the library, you have to tell your reader that—with much prettier language, preferably.

The first and easiest part of this is showing the time. This can be done in a variety of ways: describing the sunset, having the character check their watch, mentioning the algebra classroom, or simply stating the date.

If you're setting a scene after a time skip, you can establish the season— the sweltering summer air or blustering chill of winter. Again, we're tapping into our five senses; they serve as double duty for both grounding the character and illustrating the world around them.

The second part of this is establishing the *where*. This involves stating or describing where the character is in that moment. If this is a recurring location your readers are familiar with, stating it is sufficient; for example, "They met at the gym." But if this is a new setting the reader hasn't yet experienced, you should describe it to them so they can visualize it.

That's where things get tricky. Some writers throw themselves into describing inconsequential details that don't set the scene nearly as well as they're hoping. Here are a few pointers to help you set up the *where* without bugging your readers.

Avoid layouts

There was a desk against the back wall and a chair beside the left wall. A wardrobe stood next to the door with a bed against the right wall and an end table to its left.

A lot of writers begin setting the scene in this manner, and after reading this sentence, I'm sure you can see the issue. It's both boring and confusing. When writers give an exact layout, they're playing twister with their reader's head.

Readers envision as they're reading. They connect the dots as they go. When you start putting dressers to the left and closets to the right, you're rearranging the furniture they've already established in their mind.

Additionally, saying the exact placement of furniture doesn't communicate what a location looks like. I know there's a wardrobe next to the door, but I have no idea what the wardrobe or the door looks like. And does the wardrobe or the door even matter? Probably not. But the ambiance, energy, and style certainly do.

Avoid measurements

The room was 6 feet by 6 feet, and the ceiling was 15 feet high with wood paneling about 6 inches in width.

This isn't a riveting description. It's a blueprint. Lots of writers revert to listing exact measurements when setting a scene, and it's a big mistake.

First, measurements are not important. No one is whipping out their ruler alongside your novel, trying to envision the exact size of the character's bedroom. Second, like the last point, it's boring as all hell to read. But most importantly, measurements tell the reader nothing of value about the setting. Remember, ambiance and style are what matter, not square footage.

When it comes to measurements, this is the perfect time to use generalizations. Is it a small bedroom, or a grand bedroom? In just one word, you can tell the reader everything they need to know about the size of the space the character has entered. Now you can move on to more valuable descriptors.

Colors, texture, and material

This will transport your readers and give them the visual they crave. They don't care if the wardrobe is next to the doorway. What they care about is the color of the wardrobe or the material it's made of. Is it rustic mahogany polished to a shine? Is it weathered and neglected, with faded olive green paint chipping at the hinges?

No one cares about the height of the walls. Instead, tell the reader that the walls are a sterile, stark white, or that the buckling wallpaper is spattered with browning blood.

These are descriptors that will linger in your reader's mind, in large part because they tap into the five senses. Texture is touch. Color and material are sight. But these details are also transportive and engaging. Colors create an emotional response in people, and material like wood or marble can dictate era or tone.

Relinquish a bit of control

The reason so many writers struggle with setting the scene is because of their deep need to control the readers. They want to make sure their readers envision the scene perfectly, exactly as the writer intended.

I've got some bad news for you. You can be as thorough as you'd like, but your readers are still going to interpret your work the way they want to, based on personal experience and bias.

Let go of the need to have everyone interpret your setting in the exact manner you see it. I promise, even if you describe every minute detail, people are going to have their own vision. That's not to say you should throw in the towel and abandon describing anything at all. That would make for a lackluster reading experience. But it's important to give the most engaging descriptions and leave the smaller, less important bits to the reader's imagination.

This need for control is what encourages writers to make a lot of scene-setting mistakes, like excessive world-building that doesn't benefit the story, or those stupid measurements and layouts. Instead, focus on creating beautiful and transportive imagery. Readers will feel much more connected to your story, which is exactly what you want.

THE SCENE'S INTENTION

We've reached the final step in setting the scene: clarifying its intention. Sometimes people call this establishing the character's goal, needs, or conflict.

This is usually the last thing referenced when setting the scene. You've already established the perspective, time, and location, and now you must confirm the intention. This requires digging into the emotion of your character, as it often directly translates to their goal or conflict.

For example, if your character wakes up in a dungeon, their goal is probably figuring out why they're there, what happened to them, or how to get out. You can easily establish this goal in several ways.

Narrative

This is the most obvious choice. You can simply explain the character doesn't know where they are or why they're there. Immediately, the intention becomes clear: getting them the hell out of that dungeon.

Beware, if you go with this option, be sure to keep things interesting. It can be all too easy to fall into *telling* the readers a problem rather than *showing* it, which isn't exactly the most entertaining way to write.

Dialogue

Maybe the character whispers, "What the fuck?"

This lets readers know they have no idea where they are, and that in itself is the conflict.

Inner monologue

This choice utilizes the character's thoughts. They can think to themself, *Where am I?*

Again, we are presenting the reader with the goal, which is to figure out where they are.

With all these tools at hand, you should be able to seamlessly set any scene in your novel.

Please note, setting the scene doesn't need to be a long process. You can often accomplish this task in a sentence or two. Don't bore your reader with a lengthy grounding process before diving into the scene itself. In my opinion, if setting the scene takes longer than a paragraph or two, you're probably rambling.

Next, we move onto pacing your novel.

SUMMARY

SETTING THE SCENE

- To set the scene you need to determine the character's perspective, the when and where, and the intention of the scene.

- The character's perspective:

  - Name the character.
  - Try to use the five senses to describe the location and the character's feelings.
  - Establish a tone or energy for the scene.

- The when and where:

  - When: What is the time of day, date, or season?
  - Where: What is the location?
  - Avoid descriptions of strict layouts and measurements of the size, shape, and contents of a space.
  - Instead, describe the color, texture, and materials of the space to dictate tone and create an emotional response.

- The intention of the scene:

- Establish the character's goal, their needs, or their conflict using narrative, dialogue, and inner monologue.

CHAPTER 13
PACING YOUR NOVEL
WHEN TO TAKE IT SLOW OR MOVE THINE ASS

THE PACING of a story refers to the rhythm and flow of your novel. How fast or slow is the plot moving? That right there is your book's pace.

Pacing is relevant in multiple aspects of the writing process. Have you written a fast-paced or a slower-paced book? Typically, novels with any type of adventure tend to be on the faster side, whereas something like literary fiction might have a slower pace.

Next, we look at our novel on a scene-by-scene basis. Even if your book is mostly fast-paced or slow-paced, each scene you write is going to have its own movement and flow. Some scenes will be quicker than others; that's perfectly normal and in fact encouraged. You don't want your novel to feel like a continuous series of fast scenes because then your content will seem rushed and exhausting. But in most cases, you also don't want your story to be continuously slow because, well, that's boring.

Instead, your novel should be a series of low and high points as well as slow and fast points weaving in and out of one another. Remember the Roller-Coaster Method? Yup, we're utilizing it again.

Take a look at your outline. Are there too many fast points with zero interruption? If that's the case, fiddle with the structure and see if you can break it up with something slower. Give your reader a moment's peace. But if you have too many slow scenes in a row—and the genre doesn't necessarily call for slowness—it's time to break up the monotony with some spice.

If you're unsure how to pace a particular scene, consider the character's point of view. A lot of writers get so caught up in their own head, they forget to think about the character's experience. If you were in their position, how would the moment feel to you? If a scene feels slow to the character, it's appropriate for the pace to be slow as well. Alternatively, if the moment feels fast, the pacing should reflect that.

Here's an easy rule to follow: Fight scenes, chases, battles, explosions, and raids are all heart-pumping moments, which means we're looking at some fast-paced scenes. Unless the character is in shock, experiencing the carnage in slow motion, or their life is flashing before their eyes, you're going to want to write these scenes with speed in mind.

Now, let's consider which scenes should unfold slowly. What sort of moments happen slowly in real life? Monotony is probably at the top of the list, but remember, our goal is to engage the reader, not bore them. What about happiness? Romance? Pleasure? The moments that are so good, you want to hang onto every detail. If your character feels this way, the reader probably wants those details too. Alternatively, sometimes tragedy seems to make time stop, and you may want to reflect that in your work. Whether your character is having the orgasm of a lifetime, or they just learned their father died, these are both instances when a slower pace may suit the scene perfectly.

There are several ways to manipulate pace to your advantage.

Sentence structure

Sentence structure can do a world of good or a whole lot of damage to the pacing of a scene. The general rule is that longer sentences go in slower paced scenes, and shorter sentences go in fast scenes.

This doesn't mean you only use short sentences in fast scenes and long sentences in slow scenes. That would make your faster scenes repetitive and robotic, while your slower scenes would read as rambling and complicated. It's important to vary your sentence structure throughout the entirety of your novel. But the idea is to use sentence structure to your benefit on a scene-by-scene basis.

No one's saying you can't have a few long sentences in a fast scene or a few short sentences in a slow scene. Mix up the length, but put a bit more focus on the structure that suits your scene best.

The devil's in the details

Much like sentence structure, if you're writing a slower scene, you elaborate on the details. If you're writing a fast scene, you rein them in.

If your character is experiencing one hell of a kiss, this is usually a slower, sensual moment. Take your time describing the feeling of their lips pressed together, their heart rate, and their wavering breathing.

If you were to give the same amount of detail to a fight scene, the readers would get bored and a little confused. This is an issue that a lot of writers have when it comes to action. They feel the need to describe every movement, maneuver, and detail. All this does is slow the scene to a glacial pace, which eliminates the tension of the battle at hand.

Remember your character's point of view. Fight scenes move fast, so the character isn't going to remember each movement or notice every detail. Focus on the most visceral components and save the word dumps for the slower scenes.

Conversations

If your characters are having a relaxed conversation, this will probably require a slower pace. You can take advantage of this by adding narrative to the mix. Describe their body language, their facial expressions, or the changes to the setting around them. This is also an opportunity to use longer sentences to keep the pace on point.

If the dialogue is firing off—for example, a heated argument—you'll probably want to utilize a fast pace. That means the narrative should be kept to a minimum. Tell the reader what they absolutely need to know, like who is speaking or any relevant actions. Body language and facial expressions should be written sparingly and only when they paint a very important visual. This is a great time to use some shorter sentences to keep the conversation flowing quickly.

Show versus tell

The slower the pace, the more you want to show. Conversely, the faster the pace, the more you want to tell.

This doesn't mean a bloody battle or gun fight should be all tell, no show. But when the details don't matter, you can give the reader a brief tell as a transition and move on to the good stuff.

It's also important to note that transitions as a whole typically rely on telling. Sure, your character's school life may not be pertinent to the plot, but sometimes it must be mentioned for the sake of realism. They may be slaying vampires, but they're still a teenager with finals next week. This would be an appropriate time to tell the reader this information in brief transitions, then keep it moving.

Focus on moving your story from plot point to plot point. If weeks happen in between, then explain it in a short transition—a paragraph at most. Your characters have lives outside the story, and the reader appreciates you acknowledging it, but they also don't care.

We'll cover more about show versus tell in Chapter 21.

Cliffhangers

The goal behind pacing is to keep the reader interested without having long lulls or rushing the content. Ending the chapter with a cliffhanger is the perfect way to address both issues.

The reader isn't going to want to put the book down after a cliffhanger, because they need to know what happens next. This is an effective way to keep the story moving.

Please keep in mind, a cliffhanger doesn't have to be life-and-death. It also doesn't have to have a fast pace. A cliffhanger could be a conversation ending in a surprising way or an unexpected kiss. Implementing cliffhangers at the end of your chapters will help with the overall pace of your novel, whether the scene it concludes is fast or slow.

Pay attention to pacing throughout the writing process. Make sure you're using appropriate sentence structures and details that fit the scene. Next up, we're breaking down the book even further by analyzing subplots.

SUMMARY

PACING YOUR NOVEL

- Pacing refers to the movement of the story. It's the rhythm and flow of your novel, and whether it reads as fast or slow.

- Your novel should be a roller coaster of low points and high points as well as slow points and fast points weaving in and out of one another.

- If you're unsure how to pace a particular scene, consider the character's experience and if the moment is slow or quick for them.

- Tips for manipulating pace:

  - Longer sentences create a slower pace. Shorter sentences create a faster pace. But be sure to vary sentence length overall.
  - More details imply a slower pace, while fewer details equate to a faster pace.
  - Adding narrative to conversations slows the pace of the scene, while keeping narrative to a minimum can add quickness to a dialogue exchange.
  - The slower the pace, the more you want to show. Conversely, the faster the pace, the more you may need to tell.
  - Adding cliffhangers to the ends of chapters keeps the story interesting while losing any chance of lulls.

CHAPTER 14
SUBPLOTS

THE SIDE QUESTS OF YOUR MIGHTY NOVEL

A SUBPLOT IS a secondary plot within your novel. Sure, your main character is saving the world, but maybe along the way she falls in love. That romance is your subplot—a smaller story that occurs alongside the primary focus, enhancing the overall plot but never overtaking it.

The subplot isn't the basis of the story. You're not going to see it featured in any depth in the back-of-the-book blurb, and it certainly won't get more page time than the plot. But that doesn't mean it's unimportant. Subplots add depth to a story and realism to your characters, making the story meatier and juicier. In fact, there are a ton of benefits to subplots, and we're going to cover just a few of them now.

WHY YOU SHOULD INCLUDE SUBPLOTS

They deepen characterization

In most novels, your protagonist has a problem, they try to solve it, and they're often victorious in the end. This doesn't tell us a whole lot about the protagonist, does it? If we're only seeing one side of the character, we're not getting a good look at other aspects of their life and personality.

Providing a well-rounded look at your protagonist is extremely important because that's what makes your audience relate to them. If your reader doesn't connect with the character, they're not going to care what happens to them. Why would anyone give a shit that your main character needs a wedding date if they don't like her, let alone know much of anything about her?

Enter subplots. They give the protagonist an opportunity to showcase multiple sides of their personality. Most subplots revolve around relationships (romance, friendships, familial, etc.) and allow you to illustrate how this person behaves in various situations with different people. Say your rugged hero is battling space monkeys in your action-packed sci-fi adventure. The reader already gets to see his gritty, courageous side, but his romantic subplot provides further depth and reveals his softness and sensitivity.

That's the beauty of the subplot. It gives you the opportunity to expand on your character and make them infinitely more likeable, while adding layers and dimension.

They add variety

If you're writing romance, your plot will likely be passionate, or sweet and fluffy. If you're writing an adventure, your plot is going to be gripping and tense. These are all good things, but too much of a good thing can get old. Subplots provide the relief you need by breaking up the plot with something new and refreshing.

Remember the Roller-Coaster Method? Subplots can add some lows to your highs and vice versa. If you're writing a romance, a subplot featuring strife between the main character and their best friend could punctuate the steamy scenes. Subplots are there to mix up the monotony of whatever weight your main plot carries through the story.

They mirror the themes

Many writers weave a message into their story. They have themes they want to communicate or a pearl of wisdom they'd like to share. Your main plot is your primary avenue for getting this point across, but subplots can easily promote your themes as well.

Say the message you're trying to promote is to stick it to the man. Your protagonist lives in a corrupt society, and she's plotting to take down the evil king subjugating the masses. Maybe her father is a loyalist who vehemently disagrees with her mission. By the end of the book, our heroine is not only able to defeat the king, but she finally stands up to her father and claims her independence. Just like that, you've reinforced your message while also adding depth to your character's journey.

They add realism

In my opinion, this is the most important reason to include subplots. People live complicated lives. No matter what goal we're pursuing, there will inevitably be things that get in the way or situations that require our attention. Some of us have issues with our family. Some of us go to work or school. Some of us fall in and out of love. Implementing these elements into your story will make your characters' lives much more realistic and relatable.

Additionally, a lot of writers like to concoct wild, improbable stories. We write about monsters, aliens, fairies, and other things that—supposedly—don't exist. If your story is filled with the fantastical and far-fetched, it's nice to add some realism to the mix. That's what subplots are for.

As we already covered, subplots usually revolve around character dynamics and bonds, like a failing marriage or an estranged relationship between a father and son. These kinds of problems add authenticity to an otherwise unbelievable story. Vampires and werewolves don't feel that implausible if, in between the glitter and shifting, someone's fighting with their mother or embarrassing themselves in front of their crush.

Now that I've convinced you to include a subplot or two (you're welcome), let's cover the common mistakes you'll want to steer clear of during the writing process.

MISTAKES TO AVOID WHEN WRITING SUBPLOTS

Distancing the subplot too far from the plot

Your plot and subplots need to be connected in some way. If your subplot doesn't have an impact on the plot, it shouldn't be there at all. Without some type of tether, the subplot will feel shoehorned in, as if the author added it without thought or purpose.

For example, if your story is about a princess reclaiming her kingdom, all subplots must be tied to her quest. Say you'd love to give her a romantic subplot. How can we tie it to her goal? Perhaps she falls in love with a soldier helping her cause. This directly relates to the plot because now she and her love interest are reclaiming her kingdom together. Maybe she falls for the enemy. This will clearly complicate the plot, as her goal and her heart are now in direct opposition.

One of the points of a subplot is to introduce something new and interesting to the story. You don't want to break up the excitement with filler, and a subplot with no relation to the plot will come across as just that. Sure, subplots typically aren't as engaging as the actual plot, but they should be entertaining in their own way and should serve an easily identifiable purpose.

In this example, both subplot options have a clear intention. The first one creates a unified team fighting for the same cause, whereas the second one makes the plot much more difficult.

Too many subplots

Many stories are complicated, but you don't want to over-complicate your novel with too many subplots. Sometimes writers think a buttload of subplots adds even more depth to their book, but really, they're confusing readers and creating more chances for error. When you have a ton of subplots to manage, it can be easy to let a few fall through the cracks.

Reading fiction can sometimes be challenging, but it should always be entertaining. It should never feel like work, because if it does, readers are going to put the book down.

Subplots that overtake the plot

This one should be self-explanatory. Has your subplot overpowered the plot? You can tell if that's the case because there are more scenes or chapters devoted to the subplot than to the plot itself. Another mistake is when writers focus on the plot at the beginning and end of the novel but use the entire midsection to showcase the subplots. This is a major problem.

If your subplot overtakes your plot, it's time to have an honest conversation with yourself. What book do you really want to write? Maybe your plot is about an alien invasion, but the romantic subplot has taken centerstage. Perhaps this is your sign to write a romance instead. Hell, sci-fi romance is a thing. Write *that* book.

Subplots that go nowhere

Like your plot, your subplots need to be resolved by the end of the book. We need an explanation, and the arc needs to come to fruition.

If one of your subplots involves a friendship on the rocks, something must come of it. If the issue is left unresolved, it'll serve as a huge distraction from the plot. What was the point of the subplot if it went nowhere? Why include it only for it to disappear unanswered? These are the questions your readers will ask, and rightfully so.

Of course, there are exceptions to the rule, mainly when you're writing a series. If you're writing a book series, it's common for portions of the plots and subplots to continue from one book to the next. If you don't resolve the strained friendship in book one, readers will assume it will be resolved in book two. But if you don't plan on addressing it later in the series, you better wrap it up in this manuscript before moving on.

Next, we're going to talk about the dreaded sagging middle syndrome.

SUMMARY

SUBPLOTS

- A subplot is a secondary plot within your novel. They're important for many reasons, including:

- Deepening the characterization by showing multiple sides of your character's personality.
- Adding variety, as they break up the plot with something new and refreshing.
- Mirroring the themes in the story. Even though your plot is the primary avenue for getting the theme across, subplots can easily promote your theme as well.
- Adding realism to your novel. Since we all live complicated lives, it makes sense that your characters will too. Subplots make your story relatable to the reader.

- Mistakes to avoid when writing subplots:

- Distancing the subplot from the plot. The plot and subplots need to be connected in some way.
- Too many subplots that confuse both the reader and writer.
- Subplots that overtake the main plot, turning the book into something else entirely.

- Unresolved subplots. Like your main plot, your subplots need to be resolved by the end of the book.

CHAPTER 15
SAGGING MIDDLE SYNDROME

THOSE SAGGY, DRAGGY, BORING BITS

MANY WRITERS PUT little thought into the middle of their story. They might have an incredible inciting incident or a super exciting climax, but in between these two points, the characters are just going through the motions and meandering through life. This forces the reader to slog through the story, hoping to reach a worthwhile end—or worse, they put the book down altogether. This issue is known as sagging middle syndrome (SMS). Not all writers struggle with this, but it's certainly common enough to have a fun nickname.

It's easy for the middle of a novel to be overlooked by the writer because we tend to associate intrigue and excitement with the beginning, when the action commences, and when everything comes to a head at the end. But your book needs to be engaging throughout. You can't get away with a series of mundane, inconsequential events stuffed into the middle of your story.

Now that I've instilled in you a fear you probably didn't have beforehand (sorry about that), I'm here to make sure the middle of your story is just as impactful as the rest of it. The goal is to entertain your readers from the first page to the last, and implementing these tips will allow you to do just that.

Structure

Refer to the structural diagram in Chapter 2. See how the middle of the plot is called the rising *action*? That means stuff needs to happen—preferably interesting stuff.

It's common for new writers to dive straight into the writing process with zero concept of structure. Writing is fun, and it's easy to get excited about your story. Unfortunately, this knee-jerk reaction will come back to haunt you.

As we've covered, structure is the framework of your novel. It's a series of events in a specific order that allows the writer to tell their story in the most effective, logical, and entertaining way possible. You have multiple structural models to choose from, like in medias res or the Hero's Journey, and you have the wiggle room to break free and devise your own model based on storytelling standards. But you absolutely *must* utilize some kind of structure. Otherwise, SMS is almost certainly inevitable.

Think of your novel as a human body, and the structure is the skeleton. You have the inciting incident, which are the femurs, and the climax, which is the skull. If you have no structural points in the middle, then your story cannot support itself; it would be a mushy blob, like Jabba the Hutt but even less appealing.

Before you start writing, familiarize yourself with storytelling structure. Research the structural elements that make up the spine of your novel, and follow them in order to avoid SMS well before putting pen to page —or fingers to keyboard.

Outlining

If you've been following this book so far, you should already have an outline ready, or at the very least be planning to create one soon. You may be averse to this step, but an outline shows you the entire story in shorthand, so you can pinpoint issues and fix them ahead of time.

This is especially relevant to SMS. If a third of your novel is uneventful, it's going to be very apparent in your outline and quite easy to tackle. You've got the whole story laid out in front of you, and you should be able to see the exact point when everything slows down enough to lull readers to sleep. Now you can isolate that section and rebuild it before you've even written it, which saves you a ton of time.

Break your character's legs

Not literally.

Well . . . maybe literally.

Plots revolve around conflict. Whether your character has a goal or a dilemma, they must face opposition before reaching the climax. Worsening the character's problem is the perfect way to both raise the stakes and avoid SMS.

The middle serves two purposes. You're bringing the character closer to the climax, and you're making their journey harder along the way. Whatever it takes to make this road as tough as possible, do it. Lay them off their job, kill their parents, reveal a traitor, or destroy their home. Look, writers don't exactly have the most angelic reputation, so take this opportunity to showcase your devilish ways.

If you're not convinced, I'm going to bring up structure once again. The rising action is specifically designed to increase tension and suspense for the sake of the climax. Other, more specific structural events that occur in the middle of the novel are **the complication**, **the crisis**, and **the breaking point**.

The complication is an event that makes the plot even more complicated, as the name suggests. In *The Savior's Champion*, the complication is when Tobias realizes he doesn't have feelings for the woman he's competing to marry, but instead is falling for her sister.

The crisis is a major conflict or catastrophe that hits the protagonist hard. It's often referred to as the "mini climax," and it usually results in a huge loss for the main character or a tremendous failure on their part.

Then we have the breaking point, which is the lowest point in the novel for your main character. Something terrible happens—often the crisis—and they lose all hope. They're down on themselves, and they question whether they can achieve their goal. We'll dive a little deeper into this in the next chapter, so stay tuned.

You don't need to include all these points. The crisis and the breaking point are often one and the same. Sometimes the complication leads to the crisis, and sometimes there are multiple complications and crises. The bottom line is, these structural points give you ample opportunity to make the middle of your novel an engaging read, and you do that by unapologetically kicking your main character while they're down.

Keep your subplots at bay

As we covered in the previous chapter, the subplots of your novel should never overpower the plot. That's exactly what usually happens during SMS. Say your inciting incident has your main character venturing on a quest for the Amulet of Truth. However, the middle of the novel focuses only on their bonding with friends or the world you've built around them. These elements are nice, but that's not the story your readers signed up for.

That's not to say a subplot can't dominate a scene, but it shouldn't take up over a third of your novel. If your plot is about a romance, the middle of your novel shouldn't exclusively revolve around the main character's childhood trauma.

Don't fall into the trap of overprioritizing your subplots. Keep them to the side where they belong.

Move the story forward

Every chapter needs to move the plot forward. It could be the tiniest inch, but it needs to be something. The easiest way to do this is to look at your plot through the lens of setting and achieving goals.

Your main character has an objective, like finding the Amulet of Truth. But you can't launch your character on this quest and have them immediately find the amulet. That wouldn't be any fun, right? Steps need to be taken in the middle of the story to bridge the gap between these two points.

Maybe the last person to see the amulet is a magical witch who lives in a dark, mysterious forest. Maybe the only person who can navigate this forest is the main character's ex-boyfriend. Just like that, you've found your complication. Your protagonist is forced to make a dangerous journey with their lousy, piece-of-shit ex. Imagine all the entertaining drama that could ensue with these two characters at each other's throats while simultaneously depending on one another to survive.

Say our bickering duo find the witch, and she gives them an enchanted map to the amulet that can only be read by the light of a dragon's flame. Looks like your main character needs to find a dragon now. And not only are dragons notoriously violent, but our poor protagonist is allergic to their scales. Instantly, another complication arises.

Notice how each of these steps brings your character closer to their goal while also providing entertaining content for the middle of the story. That's exactly what you should aim for when crafting your novel's rising action. Take your protagonist forward one inch at a time, and do it in a manner that increases engagement, raises the stakes, and of course, avoids SMS.

Now that you've given your middle a much-needed makeover, let's talk a bit more about the breaking point.

SUMMARY

SAGGING MIDDLE SYNDROME

- Sagging middle syndrome (SMS) is when the middle of the novel lacks depth and fails to move the story forward in an interesting manner.

- How to avoid SMS:

- Before you start writing, take a look at the structural elements that make up the backbone of your story.
- An outline shows you the entire story in shorthand, so you can pinpoint issues and fix them. Isolate the saggy section and rebuild it before you've even written it.
- Story plots revolve around conflict. Worsen whatever problem your character is dealing with.
- Structural events that occur within the middle of the novel are the complication, the crisis, and the breaking point.
- The complication is an event that makes the conflict even more complicated.
- The crisis is a major conflict that results in a huge loss for the protagonist. This is often referred to as the "mini climax."
- The breaking point is the lowest point in the novel for the main character. Something terrible happens, and they lose all hope.

- The subplots of a novel should never overpower the main plot.
- Every chapter needs to move the plot forward. Look at your plot through the lens of setting and achieving a goal.

CHAPTER 16
THE BREAKING POINT
MAKING YOUR AUDIENCE CRY
SAD READER TEARS

THE BREAKING POINT is a monumental scene in your novel. Something devastating happens to your main character, and much like the title implies, they break down. Usually, this is a hard blow that works against the goal they're trying to achieve.

This event occurs right before the climax, as its entire purpose is to raise the stakes and fuel that part of the story. Being the sadistic writer you are, you want your protagonist to lose hope; and you want your reader to be angry and devastated alongside them right before the conflict comes to a head.

But Jenna! I've never heard of the breaking point before . . .

Like menstruation, it goes by many names. Sometimes it's called "the crisis," "the black moment," or "all is lost." Different structures call this plot point different things, but they all basically mean the same thing.

Most genres have a breaking point. In romance novels, the breaking point almost always involves a breakup, an argument, or some type of estrangement. In crime fiction, the breaking point is often when the lead detective is suspended or removed from their big case. Breaking points vary in intensity because they depend on the stakes of each individual story. Fighting with a friend can just as easily trigger a breaking point as the death of a loved one depending on the genre and conflict of the novel.

The breaking point is often cited as one of the most important plot devices because all that drama and emotion will make the protagonist's inevitable triumph—i.e., the climax and resolution—so much more satisfying. Giving your character a major failure right before their conflict comes to a head raises your stakes to the highest level, which is exactly what you need going into the climax. These two plot points paired together will make the character's success feel satisfying and well-deserved.

You may think you have the breaking point figured out, and maybe you do. But unfortunately, there are quite a few misconceptions about the breaking point that we need to bust open first.

Myth #1: The breaking point is optional

Sure, the breaking point is optional. Writing a good book is optional as well.

While it's completely up to you whether you include any structural elements in your story, they exist for a reason: because they work. You'll see breaking points in nearly all pieces of fiction. Some are more dramatic than others, depending on the story's conflict, but I've yet to read a full-length novel or watch a movie that didn't include some type of fall from grace. We all love to be the exception to the rule, but this is one of those times when you would be standing out for the wrong reasons.

Myth #2: The breaking point can appear anywhere

Nope.

The breaking point *must* occur right before the climax—maybe a chapter or two prior. If you're using the Three-Act Story Structure, the breaking point is often referred to as "The Break into Act III." The climax is usually the most adrenalized moment in the book, so having your character transition from being completely hopeless to working their ass off to achieve their goal is very appealing to the reader. We don't enjoy stories about people who easily achieve their goals because most of us can't relate. Struggle, effort, and tenacity make a character's triumph feel earned. The breaking point does double duty for the author because it both emotionally devastates the reader and also plants seeds toward an epic climax. You need to heighten those stakes as much as possible, and the breaking point is the way to do it.

Simply put, if you put your breaking point anywhere else in the novel, it defeats its entire purpose.

Myth #3: The breaking point is the lowest point in the protagonist's life

This can be true, but it doesn't have to be. The breaking point is the main character's lowest point *in the plot*. Whether their lowest point in the plot is the same as their lowest point in life is up to you, but they certainly don't have to be one and the same.

Maybe their backstory was absolute hell. That doesn't matter, because the book is not about their backstory. The breaking point is the part of your novel's plotline when your main character is at their emotional worst.

Now that you know all about breaking points, and why they're super-duper important, how do you write an effective one?

Tie it to the plot

A good breaking point is linked to the plot or goal of the story. Whatever tragedy the protagonist experiences, it needs to make their conflict feel insurmountable.

Say you're writing a crime thriller about a cop trying to solve a murder case. If her breaking point is losing her brother to cancer, that's super sad, but it's got nothing to do with the plot. However, if the murderer in question kills the protagonist's brother, that's a much more effective breaking point. It's linked directly to the plot, and it'll evoke an enormous amount of guilt in our dutiful cop. She took the case and put her brother at risk.

As we've covered, a good breaking point needs to be both emotional for the reader as well as the character. But it still needs to have a direct link to the plot if it's going to make any sense to the story at hand.

Utilize your main character's weaknesses

What is your protagonist afraid of losing most? Make them lose it.

What is their deepest shame? Expose it.

That is why romance novels often feature a split or estrangement as the breaking point. The story revolves around a relationship, so taking it away would naturally be devastating. Additionally, these breakups are often due to the protagonist's weaknesses or insecurities. Maybe they fear abandonment, which causes them to leave relationships prematurely. Maybe they're ashamed their lover will learn something terrible about them, which is why they push them away.

This is also why death or near-death experiences are commonly utilized in breaking points, especially in adventure-based stories. If someone close to the protagonist dies or almost dies due to the hero's endeavors, the main character will naturally feel significant guilt for their role in the situation. What did they do wrong to cause such a tragedy? How can that mistake or death be directly linked to their fears or shame?

Give your main character a (brief) time to mourn

Whether it's through anger, rage, tears, or regression, the reader needs to see your protagonist at a new emotional low. Your character has spent the entirety of the book fighting toward a singular goal. Now, they're taking a step back. Something significant must've happened for them to have such an extreme change in behavior, and you can emphasize the significance of the breaking point through the character's emotional state.

How the character initially reacts to the breaking point is going to depend on the context, but typically, they react poorly. In hero stories, especially ones that involve a team, the main character usually quits or leaves the crew entirely. In coming-of-age stories, the protagonist typically turns away from their friends, secluding themselves. You may write the character sobbing over a carton of ice cream, drowning their sorrows in alcohol, or simply being a depressed blob, unwilling to leave their bedroom. Whatever their manner of mourning is, show it to the reader.

That is why the breaking point usually occurs one or two chapters before the climax as opposed to directly before the climax. Readers need a bit of time to see just how emotionally fucked your character is. Make it impactful for the reader, but don't drag it out. A scene or two will get the job done.

Give your main character a reason to shake off their funk

The breaking point can't last forever. We're rocketing toward the climax, and we need that protagonist ready to go ASAP. After a bit of wallowing, another plot point must occur that reignites their desire to achieve their goal. Sometimes this plot point makes them feel stupid for straying from the goal in the first place, and they're now filled with the overwhelming urge to redeem themselves.

Using the hero example, maybe the enemy attacks, and the hero realizes how deeply they're needed. In a romance novel, the protagonist could learn their lover is moving across the country, and the idea of them slipping away is too much to bear. Think of the breaking point as the ashes your phoenix character must rise from. After breaking, they need to gather themselves and head for the climax despite their weakened state.

Now that we've covered the breaking point, you may think it's time to dive into the climax. Not yet! First, let's shake things up in the next chapter with plot twists.

SUMMARY

THE BREAKING POINT

- The breaking point is a device in your novel where something devastating happens to your main character and they break down.

- Common misconceptions of the breaking point:

- *The breaking point is optional.* You will see a breaking point in nearly all pieces of fiction. Some are more dramatic than others depending on the stakes.
- *The breaking point can appear anywhere.* It must occur right before the climax in order to serve its purpose to the story.
- *The breaking point is the lowest point in the main character's life.* This can be true, but it doesn't have to be. The breaking point is the lowest point for your main character in the plot.

- How to write an effective breaking point:

- A good breaking point is linked to the plot or goal of the story.
- What is your main character afraid of losing most? Make them lose it. What is their greatest shame? Expose it.
- The reader needs to see the character at a new emotional low. This could be through anger, rage, sadness, regression, etc. Make it impactful, but don't drag it out.

- After a bit of wallowing, another plot point must occur that reignites their desire to achieve their goal.

CHAPTER 17
PLOT TWISTS

WELL, I DIDN'T SEE THAT
COMING . . .

I'M a huge fan of plot twists because they have the power to take any story to a new level. A good book will leave you feeling awed and inspired, but a good book with a great plot twist will blow your mind.

A plot twist is a drastic change in the plot or direction of a novel. Writers use them to surprise their readers and keep them interested in the story. A well-done twist will leave readers wondering, *How did I not see this coming?* Twists introduce new characters or conflicts, reveal that a seemingly resolved problem has only just begun, or expose that someone or something isn't quite as it seems.

Not every book needs a plot twist, but they're tons of fun when appropriate. Certain genres are expected to have plot twists—for example, thrillers and horror novels—whereas other genres, while twisty, are often considered less surprising. For example, the plot twist in a romance novel is usually relatively predictable, seeing as the genre requires a happily ever after (HEA). Whatever the twist, we know our leading couple is going to end up together in love.

Herein lies the struggle: To twist or not to twist. A lot of writers know exactly where their story needs to go but worry it's too stagnant or predictable. Do they throw in a plot twist, or are they overthinking the process?

Honest answer? It depends. Sometimes certain story elements are predictable, and there's not much you can do about it. Some writers can totally surprise the reader and kill off their protagonist, but other writers need the protagonist to win the battle. They need the hero to land the hot girl or the beefcake guy, and the readers will undoubtedly see it coming.

Furthermore, some elements *should* be predictable. If readers have no idea who the love interest of your romance novel is, that doesn't mean you're a sneaky, stealthy writer—it means your characters have zero chemistry, which is a big problem.

It's fine to give in to reader expectations for the benefit of the overall story. But it's also fan-fucking-tastic to throw in a well-placed, novel-enhancing twist. Maybe the hero lands the hottie but in a way the readers hadn't seen coming. This is the power of the plot twist. It can take the most predictable story and still make it exciting and unexpected.

How do you prepare a plot twist? I'm glad you asked . . .

Breadcrumbs

Readers aren't supposed to see a plot twist coming, but that's not the end of it. A powerful twist will leave readers scratching their heads and thinking, *It all makes sense now.*

You don't just want to surprise the reader—you want to answer a question the readers may not have had in the first place.

Achieving this effect requires proper foreshadowing, though I like to refer to it as leaving breadcrumbs—teeny tiny hints scattered throughout the text that lead to the upcoming twist. The trick is to make these hints subtle, something readers won't dwell on in the moment. However, once the plot twist hits, suddenly those hints become loud and glaring, leaving readers wondering how they missed them in the first place.

The easiest way to make these hints fly under the radar is to scatter them in scenes and interactions where the reader's attention is directed elsewhere. If the spotlight of the scene is on romance, danger, or humor, nestle an itty-bitty hint amid the dialogue. If your characters are in the thick of battle, briefly drop a hint as an afterthought while your readers are captivated by the action.

Let's lean into that battle scene idea. Say your main character has a romantic rendezvous with an unknown masked man with long hair and brown eyes. This man ends up being a soldier in her enemy's army—a plot twist for a future chapter. Right now, she's in the heat of war, fighting helmeted soldier after soldier. You could simply and *briefly* mention one of the soldiers narrowing his brown eyes as he launches his sword at her. Those two words—brown eyes—act as a breadcrumb, a mere blip within an otherwise intense, chaotic scene.

This isn't always as easy as it seems. Sometimes writers can be about as subtle as a hammer. I once read a story that went something like this:

She wove through the crowd toward the churro stand. A mysterious man in a black T-shirt bumped into her shoulder. She rubbed her shoulder, expecting an apology from the mysterious man, but he said nothing. She continued toward the churro stand, forgetting completely about the man in the black T-shirt.

Gee, I wonder if the man in the black T-shirt is going to matter at some point. Did I mention he's mysterious?

Not sure if your breadcrumbs are flying under the radar? Time to enlist some beta readers. Through their feedback, you'll be able to tell if your hints were subtle enough. If a beta reader points directly to a hint and asks, "What the hell was that about?" that's not a good sign. If you ask for their predictions, and they predict the exact plot twist you've planned, that's also not a good sign. Beta readers are going to be instrumental in telling you whether you hit or missed the mark. We'll talk more about them in Chapter 24.

The red herring

A red herring is a tool writers can use to mislead or distract their readers from a relevant clue in the story. This is also known as "redirecting suspicion," which is an especially important part of whodunnit stories.

Say you have your reader convinced the villain is the school bully. Then they get to the climax, and lo and behold, the villain is *actually* the protagonist's best friend. What the frickity frack?

Gotcha!

The trick here is to make your readers feel certain of a particular outcome. They'll think they know exactly what's going on and exactly how the story will end, but they're wrong. Cue the ominous author laughter.

If you want to convince your reader of a particular outcome, you must get them emotionally invested. If you're redirecting suspicion from the actual villain to a red herring, then the red herring character should be pretty despisable. The readers will be too caught up in their hatred to pursue other possibilities.

On the flip side, if the plot twist reveals the love interest is actually the villain, then the love interest has got to be pretty lovable. The reader will be too busy swooning to consider they're the culprit.

We've only just begun

This type of plot twist really showcases just how evil writers can be. It's also my favorite, which shouldn't be surprising.

Often, the best time to hit readers with a plot twist is when everything's calm and peaceful. The battle's won, the conflict's resolved, and your characters are feeling great.

That's your cue, oh merciless narrator. Time to rock their world.

Plot twists like this typically have the most impact when they happen at or around the climax, but they can show up at any point in the book. The key is to introduce the twist right when it seems as though the problem is solved. Finally, your cast can kick back and relax. The moment they start to decompress, it's your job to drop a crisis in their lap. Think of the worst thing that could happen in that moment and make it so.

Maybe your detective protagonist *thinks* they've arrested the killer, only for the real culprit to end up in their apartment, threatening to murder their spouse. Maybe the cyborg hero *thinks* they've defeated the alien overlord, but that six-eyed weirdo was just a henchman; the real overlord has twelve eyes and *way* more teeth.

This type of plot twist is particularly effective in any story involving danger or suspense, especially if it's a series. Mysteries, thrillers, action-adventure, horror, sci-fi, fantasy—these genres are prime real estate for these exact shenanigans. Convince the readers that a red herring, a henchman, or a mini boss is the cause of all the torture and destruction, only to reveal there's a bigger baddie waiting in the wings.

Regardless of genre, it's great to get into the habit of a bait and switch. Give your characters—and in turn, your readers—a false sense of comfort, and then pop a squat all over their hopes and dreams.

Here's what we're not going to do . . .

As fun as writing them can be, plot twists need to be handled with attention and delicacy. What we're *not* going to do is write a plot twist that's over-complicated or nonsensical.

Readers can forgive predictability, but they can't forgive a twist that makes little to no sense. You know what I'm talking about: The villain is *actually* the best friend's cousin's teacher who married the priest's grandma's dentist, and it all makes sense because they used to babysit for the hero's dog's accountant's half-sister.

We've all read that plot twist before, and I'm sure you rolled your eyes just like I did. If it barely sounds like the author understands the twist, chances are the readers won't understand—or bother to understand —either.

The same can be said with a nonsensical twist. I'm sure you've seen this kind as well. The answer to the question is something that was never once a part of the story. The villain is actually Uncle Harold. Never heard of him? That's because this is his very first mention in the plot, leaving the reader no possibility of guessing his intentions or gaining any satisfaction from his reveal.

This is entirely why you need to leave breadcrumbs throughout the story. Shocking the reader for the sake of it isn't going to generate a positive reaction. Readers will instead feel cheated, as you didn't give them a fair chance to solve the mystery. Plus, who the hell even *is* Uncle Harold? Why should anyone care if he's the bad guy?

This type of plot twist is devious and will certainly make the reader lose trust in you. They might feel like you're grasping at straws to keep their attention, or they may feel as if you made a mistake, especially if the plot twist is so far-fetched it doesn't feel like it belongs in the novel.

So go back and look at breadcrumbs, red herrings, and bait-and-switches. Keep your readers' trust while surprising the pants off of 'em.

Now that you've set up your story properly, let's not waste time getting to the climax!

SUMMARY

PLOT TWISTS

- A plot twist is a drastic change in the plot or direction of a novel. Writers use them to surprise their readers and keep them interested in the story.

- How do you prepare a plot twist?

- Scatter tiny hints throughout the text, like little breadcrumbs. The trick is to be subtle about these hints because you don't want your reader picking up on them. You want them to be surprised once the plot twist hits.
- Utilize beta readers to ensure your breadcrumbs work properly.
- The red herring is a tool writers can use that misleads or distracts the reader from a relevant clue in the story. This is also known as "redirecting suspicion." Make your readers feel certain of a particular outcome only to later prove they are wrong.
- Implement a plot twist once everything seems peaceful and resolved.
- Plot twists like this typically have the most impact when they happen at or around the climax, but they can show up at any

point in the book. The key is to utilize them right when the story calms.

- Your characters have gotten out of a difficult situation, and they're finally able to kick back and relax. Drop a worst-case scenario into their lap.

- Avoid the worst mistake when writing a plot twist: making the plot twist over-complicated or nonsensical.

- An over-complicated plot twist isn't believable, leading the reader to assume the author themselves doesn't understand their story.
- A nonsensical plot twist utilizes elements that were never featured in the novel beforehand, making it so that readers have no ability to solve the mystery on their own.

CHAPTER 18
THE CLIMAX

GET YOUR MIND OUT OF THE GUTTER

THERE ARE many orgasm jokes to be made here, but I'm putting on my professional writer hat and powering through.

The climax of a novel is when the conflict of your plot is resolved, or your protagonist's goal is achieved. This happens toward the end of the novel, right before the falling action and resolution.

Sounds simple, right? Unfortunately, it isn't. You've written an entire book surrounding this conflict, which means resolving it needs to be extremely powerful. Because of this, the climax tends to be the most exciting part of the novel. Not every climax features life-and-death stakes, but you absolutely must aim for a major impact that keeps up with the tone of your novel.

Many writers struggle with this concept. They build the suspense and anticipation, only to reach an easily resolved climax, allowing everything to fall flat.

That's not going to happen to you because you've got my nagging ass teaching you to do better. There are several tricks to writing an effective climax, and I'm giving you the inside scoop.

Give your main character a disadvantage

The climax needs to be the number one most intense moment of your novel. Nothing makes the climax—or any scene for that matter—more intense than writing the protagonist as the underdog.

You want your reader to question whether the protagonist is going to succeed. Whatever the obstacle, it cannot be a sure win. Maybe the hero enters the battle without a weapon, or their support abandoned them in the prior chapter. Maybe your leading lady hasn't prepared for her speech in the slightest.

Often, whatever disadvantage your protagonist has is a direct result of the breaking point. They quit momentarily, and now they're out of practice. They fought with their lover, and now they're spurned after making an ass of themselves. Whatever the reason, have your protagonist enter the climax as the expected loser.

This can translate into most, if not all, fiction genres. If you're writing a war story, make sure the protagonist's platoon is significantly outnumbered. If you're writing a love story, and your protagonist is fighting to win their ex-girlfriend back, make sure she's leaving town or dating someone new.

Putting your protagonist at a disadvantage is the key to ramping up the anticipation right from the start. You want your reader invested in the climax from the moment it begins to the moment it ends.

Give your obstacle an advantage

This is the antithesis of our last point. If you have a villain, they should be hamming it up and living in their prime. If the obstacle isn't sentient —for example, a record-breaking storm—it's at its worst. Whatever the obstacle, it needs to suck the absolute most at the climax.

There are few things more disappointing than when the reader gets to the climax expecting an epic showdown, and the bad guy is taken out with one swing. Even worse, the bad guy folds without a fight! Think about it from the reader's perspective: They read 300+ pages for *this*? That's like hyping up a night of bedroom magic only to pump out thirty seconds of displeasure with no happy ending.

I know, I said I'd avoid orgasm jokes, but I'm only human.

Theoretically, your protagonist has feared this villain or obstacle for the entire book. That means when they finally square off, the apprehension needs to be justified. If your reader is not intimidated by the threat, then it's time to go back to the drawing board.

The almost

In the middle of the climax, your protagonist needs to *almost* fail.

We already covered your protagonist's disadvantage and your obstacle's advantage. With these elements combined, an almost fail should be inevitable. This could be as extreme as the main character almost dying. If the stakes of your novel aren't quite so intense, it could be the main character missing the last train that could've taken them to their love interest.

Of course, this is assuming you're writing the kind of climax where the protagonist eventually succeeds. If you're writing a tragic ending, consider reversing the rule: Have the protagonist almost win. But a large chunk of stories end with some form of success, whether it's a kingdom saved or a positive lesson learned. If that's the case, your hero needs to almost fail during the climax if you want to leave the greatest impact.

This isn't just my opinion. There are tons of studies stating the almost is a vital key to a powerful climax in multiple forms of storytelling media beyond novels. Audiences respond to this method, and stories that lack the almost leave readers feeling unsatisfied.

There's a good reason for this. Readers tend to prefer protagonists who work hard for what they desire. They want to see the struggle and see the protagonist grow and push themselves. This type of journey is relatable because most people have experienced effort and failure at some point in their lives. Plus, perseverance is inspiring! So having your protagonist almost lose it all and then come back swinging is going to make your reader excited. They'll want them to succeed, and they'll feel relief and elation when they finally do.

Reveal the plot twist

As we covered in the last chapter, plot twists most often reveal themselves in the climax. This isn't a requirement, but it can certainly strengthen the stakes. If your goal is to surprise the reader, the climax is the prime place to do so.

Do you know what makes a climax that much more exciting? When the reader's expecting a right hook, and instead you knee them in the balls—metaphorically speaking, of course. And there are a million ways you can do this. Maybe the bad guy is finally revealed, and they turn out to be the protagonist's sibling. Maybe the hero is fighting to stop the evil sorcerer from obtaining the Amulet of Truth, but it turns out he had it all along.

Again, not all climaxes feature surprises, but you really ought to consider it. Even a wee little baby twist can take your climax to the next level.

Make your climax climactic

This should go without saying, but if it's here in this ole book, there's a reason for it. There's nothing more disappointing than an anticlimactic climax, and unfortunately, those are very easy to come by.

You already know the climax needs to be the most impactful moment in your novel. How do you gauge this? Here's an easy method: Look back at other exciting moments in your novel and try to surpass them. If your book features three one-on-one fight scenes, the climax should have a bigger, deadlier fight. If your romance features three swoon-worthy scenes, the climax needs to feature grand gestures that would leave your readers breathless.

This doesn't have to be the reader's favorite part of the book, but it needs to be the most intense. Melt your readers' brains and leave them wanting more.

Take your time

No one likes a quick performance.

(Last one, I promise.)

One of the worst ways to screw up your climax is making it too short. Sure, you don't want to drone on for chapters upon chapters, but this is the climax we're talking about. You need to make it count. Remember, your readers have invested a lot of time in your story, so it's your job to make it worth their while. The climax is the exact place to do this.

Fortunately, if you implement the previous steps I've listed, that should take care of this issue. Giving your protagonist a disadvantage and your obstacle an advantage means there will be lots of bumps and blunders throughout the climax, which in turn means more content. If your protagonist nearly fails, that right there is a huge moment that requires great focus. Tack on a plot twist and some exciting energy, and we're looking at a lengthy, mind-blowing climax that's sure to leave your readers satisfied.

(Okay, *that* was the last one.)

Now that you've reached the climax, let's talk about resolutions.

SUMMARY

THE CLIMAX

- The climax of a story is when the conflict of your plot is resolved, or your protagonist's goal is achieved. It usually occurs toward the end of the story.

- How to make your climax as effective as possible:

  - Give your main character a disadvantage. You want the reader to question whether the protagonist is going to succeed. This is the key to ramping up the anticipation from the start.
  - Give your obstacle an advantage. Whatever the obstacle is, it needs to suck the absolute most at the climax.
  - In the middle of the climax, your protagonist needs to almost fail.
  - Plot twists most often show up in the climax. This isn't a requirement, but it can strengthen the stakes.
  - Look back at other exciting moments in your novel and try to surpass them.
  - Don't rush the climax. The reader has invested a lot of their time in your story. Make it worth their while.

CHAPTER 19
THE END
BUT NOT REALLY

FINALLY, we've reached the resolution. Often writers confuse the climax of the book with the resolution as they both occur toward the end, but these are separate plot points with entirely different intentions. The climax is the most intense moment of your novel, when the conflict of the story comes to a head. The resolution is the final chapter of your novel—the aftermath of the climax, once everything is resolved and all questions are answered.

Think of the climax as the explosion and the resolution as the dust settling.

Writing a solid final chapter is crucial to the success of your novel because it's the last impression you're giving your readers. I've read books I thoroughly enjoyed, only to despise them after an unsatisfying ending. Your story's resolution can make or break your book in the eyes of your reader.

No pressure.

As its name suggests, the resolution requires resolving loose ends within your plot. When you write a novel, you typically introduce a conflict at the inciting incident. By the end, readers will require some sense of finality to this dilemma.

Sometimes writers get so wrapped up in world-building or character creation, they lose sight of the purpose of their story. This ultimately boils down to a lack of understanding story structure. Remember, every chapter should move the plot forward. The resolution is no different. I have read books where, by the final chapter, the conflict wasn't remotely resolved. This didn't make me feel excited about reading more from the author. It just made me feel like I wasted my time.

To avoid this, know where you're headed. You're writing the last chapter of your book. Where do you go from there? If this book is a standalone, then this is literally the end. That means every plot and subplot needs to be resolved because you've run out of words. There's nowhere else to go.

If anything isn't resolved, then it needs to be intentional. If this book is part of a series, the last chapter is the end of one plot within a much bigger story. That means you still need some type of resolution, but you'll probably leave a few remaining problems to be tackled in the sequel.

For example, the conflict of *The Savior's Champion* is whether Tobias will escape the tournament with the woman he loves. In the last chapter, this question is answered. However, a new, much bigger conflict is introduced that is explored in the sequel.

Writing a series is not a green light to leave your reader hanging. Sure, cliffhangers may abound, but big questions still need answering. Maybe the lovers are separated, or a war is beginning, but the reader at least knows the evil government's secret schemes. The goal is to resolve the underlying conflict while introducing a greater problem that incentivizes readers to pick up the sequel.

Don't forget about your subplots. Are they resolved? You don't have to wrap them all up in the last chapter specifically, but they need to have been tied up at some point along the way. Have you ever read a book where the best friend or sickly mother suddenly stops getting page time with no explanation? You noticed, and I did too. Your readers will do the same if you drop the ball on your subplots.

Of course, if you're writing a series, your subplots may continue into the sequel. That's perfectly fine and even encouraged. But try to provide a temporary finality so your readers feel satisfied in the meantime.

So, how do you create an effective resolution?

Look to your beginning

Often the resolution of your story is a mirror of your story's beginning. The resolution gives you an opportunity to show how much your characters have changed since the start.

This is particularly relevant if your protagonist has a very substantial character arc. People grow through conflict. The comparison between the start and the end of your story is going to highlight that in a big way.

In *The Savior's Champion*, the story begins with Tobias coming home to his small cottage after a long day's work. He is exhausted and overwrought with worry over the care of his family. By the end of *The Savior's Champion*, Tobias returns to this very same cottage a changed man with a new mission. His energy is different, as is his demeanor and goal. His care for his family is expressed in an entirely new way that juxtaposes the first chapter.

Don't think you have to be overt with this. No one wants to read a rambling soliloquy about how far your protagonist has come or how much they've changed. An effective ending showcases a major dichotomy between the introduction and resolution without much explanation. Trust that your readers are smart enough to pick up on the difference. If they're not, that's okay too. They'll probably enjoy the story regardless, which is all that matters.

Bring the themes home

Many stories feature a message the author is trying to convey. The resolution is the ideal time to bring this message home. The resolution is supposed to be thought-provoking and emotional, and this is largely because of themes. This is your last chance to make whatever point you're trying to make.

You don't have to be blatant about your message. In fact, you probably shouldn't be. There have been many books I absolutely loved, but once the author got to the resolution, the narrative became prolific and self-indulgent. Themes are supposed to be subtle and implied, not explicitly stated ad nauseam. Leave that for the message boards and basement dwellers. This is the last impression you're giving your readers, and you don't want it to be the taste of vomit in their mouth.

Sometimes writers treat their readers like idiots, especially in the last chapter. They're afraid readers might miss a thing or two, so they decide to spell it out for them. Don't do your readers this disservice. Allow your resolution to support your themes through its action and dialogue and trust your readers will understand. Not everyone reads books for symbology, and if that's the case, let them enjoy your story in their own way.

Satisfy the reader

If there's one goal for the resolution, it's to leave the reader feeling satisfied. They need to get what they were promised out of the novel. For example, if you're writing a romance, that means the resolution needs to have a happy ending. It's a requirement of the genre, so it's what readers expect.

But Jenna, don't I want to deliver the unexpected?

Not at the expense of ruining your book. It's great to shock readers, but surprise and outrage are not the same thing. People gravitate to certain genres with specific expectations, so pulling a 180 on your readers during the resolution isn't going to fly.

Ultimately, it's your goal to deliver on the promise of your story. Did you promise an epic romance? Give readers that happily ever after. Did you promise a gut-wrenching tragedy? The resolution should unleash buckets of tears. Write your final chapter with care and strategy, and your readers will come back for more of your books.

Avoid convenience

Convenience is your enemy in most facets of writing, but especially the resolution. You want your conflict to be resolved, but not too easily or coincidentally.

"It was all a dream," or "The answer was inside you all along." Do these lines sound familiar? They're common all-too-convenient resolutions. It's an old storytelling crutch that gives writers an easy out for the shenanigans they've created. They can write whatever they want, knowing all will be well in the end. Unfortunately, readers are often displeased with this format. They see it as a storytelling cop-out, and you better believe they won't be picking up your next book.

Utilizing a typically convenient resolution? Subvert the trope. Make the seemingly convenient into something inconvenient. Maybe the power was inside your hero all along—except it's bubbling and brewing, ready to combust. Now your hero can spend the sequel trying to extract the power before it destroys them from the inside. *That* sounds like an exciting resolution.

Shut the fuck up

Oops. Is that rude?

Look, the point of the resolution is simple: to end the story. I once read a book where the climax occurred in the middle of the story and the last one hundred pages were the resolution. It was *so* painful to read.

The resolution is supposed to resolve the story and potentially open up new questions. It's not there to introduce a new cast, expand upon the world, or show the day-to-day life of the existing characters. You may want to show the day-in-the-life of your cast, but I'm begging you to save that for an epilogue or a behind-the-scenes short story. That's not what the resolution is designed for, so stop yourself before it's too late.

Cliffhangers

I can't mention resolutions without talking about cliffhangers.

We already discussed this briefly in Chapter 13. A cliffhanger is a plot device that ends a scene suddenly and with no resolution. Basically, you put your protagonist in a precarious and sometimes dangerous situation, and you leave them there.

You've got your character cornered by a pack of dogs, or they just ran into their horrible ex-boyfriend, or they're literally hanging off a cliff. And what do you do to help them out? Nothing—at least for now.

Cliffhangers are written at the end of a scene with the intention of having them resolved in the next. They exist for the sole purpose of getting your reader to turn the page. So it may seem counterproductive to end your book with a cliffhanger. After all, there aren't any more pages to turn.

But what if you have another book coming out?

For most authors, the goal is to leave the reader feeling satisfied at the end of the novel. Ending your book with a cliffhanger produces an entirely different reaction. The point of a cliffhanger is to make your reader hungry for more. Instead of feeling satisfied, they feel anxious and eager to keep reading. This is a great asset if you happen to be writing a series.

Say you end the first book of your series with a cliffhanger. The reader may feel frustrated, but it's a *good* kind of frustration. It means they're anticipating the next installment. The key is not to assume a cliffhanger ending requires zero resolution. As we already covered, you still need to resolve your novel in some way while leaving a greater conflict open for the sequel.

It's not as hard as it sounds. Maybe the couple is happy together, but their kingdom is now launched into war. Maybe the detective solved the case but lost his job. Maybe your hero won the first intergalactic battle, but their lover was kidnapped by the enemy. In each of these situations, one problem is solved, but another has been starkly exposed.

If you're writing a standalone or the last book in a series, take a step back and think clearly. Is a cliffhanger something your audience can appreciate, or will it send them into a rage? Unless the resolution or answer is heavily alluded to, I'd wager the latter.

Oof! That was a tough one, wasn't it? Resolutions are tricky to write, but you made it through. Now that your first draft is finished, are we done?

Eh, not quite.

Brace yourself, because it's time for the self-edit.

SUMMARY
THE END

- The resolution is the very last section of your book, taking place after the climax.

- How to create an effective resolution:

  - Often the resolution of your story is a mirror of or the antithesis to the beginning. The resolution gives you an opportunity to show where your character started and how much they've changed since then.
  - This is your last chance to make whatever point you're trying to make. If you're relying on themes, the resolution should support them through the action and dialogue, not through explicit preaching.
  - If there is one goal for the resolution, it's to leave the reader feeling satisfied. They need to get what they were promised out of the novel.
  - Avoid convenience. If your conflict is eliminated too conveniently or coincidentally, your readers are going to be disappointed and unsatisfied.
  - The resolution is supposed to resolve the story and create new questions. It's not there to introduce a new cast, expand upon

the world, or show the day-to-day life of the existing characters.

- A cliffhanger is a plot device where the writing ends suddenly and with no resolution. Cliffhangers are popular for series writers, as it's common for some books in the series to end without a formal resolution.

CHAPTER 20
THE DREADED SELF-EDIT
GOD, HERE WE GO . . .

A LOT of writers finish their first draft and assume the hardest part is over. Allow me to burst your bubble; the editing phase can often take as long or longer than drafting. It's not humanly possible to create a perfect book after one attempt. When you read through your rough draft, that is going to be blatantly obvious to the point of insult—and possibly revulsion.

But Jenna, isn't it the editor's job to edit my manuscript?

Absolutely. They're supposed to edit your *manuscript*. But a rough draft isn't a manuscript. It's a pile of shit.

You can't send a rough draft to an editor. That's essentially asking them to rewrite the story for you, and that's your job, not theirs. As much as you may hate the idea, you're going to have to edit the manuscript yourself—once, twice, maybe ten or more times, until you've polished it as best you can. That's when you send it to a professional, but no sooner.

It's great to be excited about your writing journey, but now is not the time to plan your release. People who treat this as the end of the road find editing much more frustrating than it needs to be. They become discouraged by how slow the process moves, which typically leads to a rush job, imposter syndrome, anxiety, or quitting altogether. Thus, it pays to be pragmatic. This next phase can be tedious, and that's completely normal.

Many people start the self-edit, read their rough draft for the first time, and have a nervous breakdown.

But Jenna, it's so bad!

That's because it's not finished. All unfinished things are bad. Do you remember how awkward and pimply you were during puberty? You weren't finished adulting yet. The same thing's happening to your manuscript. It's about to go through all kinds of embarrassing and wonderful changes.

Pop those manuscript pimples. It'll be super gross but oh so satisfying.

The primary reason people hate editing isn't because it's difficult or time consuming. It's because it's humiliating. You have to reread your old writing, and suddenly, all those typos and inconsistencies are painfully obvious. How did you not see them sooner?

What if I told you mistakes are a good thing? They serve as evidence that you're a better writer now than you were when you first started. That's exactly what you want as a creator. You want to improve in your craft with time and experience.

You shouldn't be embarrassed each time you find a mistake. If anything, you should be relieved. There are plenty of writers who have plateaued, but you're moving forward, and that's an incredible feat.

The first draft isn't the time to worry about the intricacies of syntax and grammar, but all that changes when it comes time to edit. And while it's important to handle your self-edit in batches, eventually you're going to have to tackle these issues. You may not be an expert on commas, or maybe you struggle with passive voice. This is the time to figure that stuff out.

Starting the self-edit can be overwhelming, because oh my god, you have to edit an entire book! Except we're not going to approach it that way. Looking at the big picture is going to feel insurmountable. Instead, take the process piece by piece. You're not editing a book; you're editing a chapter. You're not completing a manuscript; you're completing the developmental changes.

Dividing your manuscript into smaller, digestible chunks is the key to tackling the self-edit with your sanity intact. Here are some appropriate steps to ensure your story and your mental stability survive the process.

READ YOUR SHITTY FIRST DRAFT

Yup. The whole damned thing. It might be embarrassing or even painful, but you can cry about it later.

Go through your manuscript chapter by chapter and read everything. Note, I didn't say *edit*. That is not the focus of this step. If you see a quick fix, like a misspelled word or a missing punctuation mark, go ahead and fix it. But ultimately your goal is to get an idea of what you're dealing with.

What are your biggest issues? What are your most repeated phrases and words? Which characters aren't capturing your attention? Which scenes need to be rewritten or axed?

You might feel like you have to fix everything right away, but if you do, I promise you'll be overwhelmed. Right now, you're getting a scope for the job ahead so you can tackle it in an organized fashion. Allow yourself this time to observe, assess, and plan for the work to come. It may make you cringe from time to time—or sentence to sentence—but it's a necessary step for turning your story into a work of art.

Tag it

While you read your first draft, you're going to notice a shit ton of . . . well, shit. Instead of editing it, we're going to tag it.

Highlight or mark any mistakes you find so future you can locate them with ease. Personally, I prefer color coding. I like to assign specific types of issues their own color. You can choose any color-coding method you'd like, as it'll depend on your style, strengths, and weaknesses. For example, you can highlight wonky grammar in blue, redundant wording in pink, and future rewrites in yellow.

Color-coding allows you to easily scroll through your document and look for specific errors to address. For instance, if you're purging repeat phrases, you can look for the pink highlight and focus your attention there.

Again, the point of tagging is to label mistakes, which makes them easier to find and fix during the self-edit.

Comments and questions

This is for the issues that can't be categorized simply by color. Maybe these mistakes are too specific, or they require a bit more thought and strategy.

Say you reach a sex scene, and it needs way more sensuous detail. Rather than stewing over it, leave a comment that states "elaborate" or "needs more detail."

This helps point your future self in the right direction while also silencing the internal overwhelm. You know the issue will be addressed eventually because you're holding yourself accountable now.

This step is also helpful if you plan to enlist critique partners. If you've got a question or problem that requires a second pair of eyes, leave a comment. Say you've written a line of dialogue, but you don't know if it's cute or cringey. Leave a comment asking exactly that, and your critique partner can answer it later.

Address inconsistencies

This is the first and only edit I recommend you make at this point. When I say inconsistencies, I mean small but meaningful changes you've decided to make that affect the entirety of the novel.

For example, are you changing a character's name, the name of a setting, or the spelling of a fantasy word? These types of edits are perfectly fine to address right now. First, because they're simple, and second, because they're really distracting. The sooner you nip 'em in the bud, the better.

It's easy to do a find and replace for these issues and make the ole switcheroo. Once you get these inconsistencies addressed, it'll feel like a major load off with little effort at all.

CREATE A LIST

After you've read your first draft, you'll have a very vivid picture of the uphill path you're about to climb. Rather than wallowing in despair or lighting the manuscript on fire, it's time to make a list. Namely, list your most common mistakes, and leave it at that.

You're not here to tally every single issue. That will only send you spiraling into a black abyss of imposter syndrome. Your goal is to list the repeat offenders so you can create an editing game plan. You've already tackled the first few major steps of the writing process, and now you want to document your problem areas. These are the areas that require the most work and education. This is not to shame you; rather, it's to give you an actionable step that will make the editing process a lot easier, while also showing you exactly where to hone your skills and grow in your craft.

If you kept a list during your drafting stage, this is the time to break it out and refer to it.

WORK BIG TO SMALL

Does that edit list feel discouraging? Don't worry; we're about to soften the blow.

First, categorize your list into three sections:

The first section will be **developmental issues**. This covers anything story related, like characterization, plot holes, or world-building.

The second section is issues with **prose**—anything regarding sentence structure, pacing, and flow.

The third section is all things **grammar and punctuation**. This phase is devoted to the nuts and bolts of our writing.

If grammar isn't your forte, no worries! Well, a little worry. It behooves you to educate yourself on the building blocks of writing so you can better your craft overall. But there are resources you can use to your advantage that can make the process easier. I recommend ProWritingAid, a grammar and style checker that will not only point out your mistakes but teach you how to avoid them in the future. It makes the self-editing process a lot less complicated, especially if you're working on issues you're not well-versed in.

You may notice these sections mirror the professional editing process, specifically the developmental, line, and copyedit. This is one hundred percent intentional. These sections categorize your large issues (developmental), the medium size issues (sentence or line level), and the smaller issues (copyedit). We will go into greater depth when we talk about working with professional editors in Chapter 25.

Please note when I say large versus small issues, I'm not referring to importance. I'm referring to the size and depth of the edit itself. You want to start with the large issues, because larger, story-based mistakes typically involve massive rewrites. It makes a lot more sense to tackle these rewrites first, then work your way down to prose and grammar after.

You may see a ton of grammatical errors from the start, but you don't have to address them if you're working on the developmental edit. Focus your attention on the phase that matters and leave the other issues for a future round.

CHAPTER BY CHAPTER

Sectioning your self-edit is vital because it creates focus. It gives you the tunnel vision you need to home in on a particular task and block out anxiety and doubt. Plus, it takes your attention away from all the other bullshit you have to work on, which makes the workload feel much more navigable.

If you have a lot of developmental issues, tackle them one at a time, starting with the one that requires the most rewrites and working your way down. Once you reach the prose and grammar sections, you can usually edit on a chapter-by-chapter basis.

Depending on how many prose and grammar issues you have, you can delegate a certain number of chapters to edit per day.

I usually give myself about three chapters per day, but that may be way too many or too few for you. Do what works best for your process. My number may be wild to you for a multitude of reasons. That's fine. I'm not the default. I encourage you to find a system that fits seamlessly into your schedule.

I know it feels insurmountable to fix up an entire manuscript, but you know what's a hell of a lot easier? Fifteen pages. Then another fifteen pages, and then another. You'll be surprised by just how quickly you can fly through your edits when you've only got one chapter at a time to worry about.

LISTEN

When you silently read the same manuscript repeatedly, you start to memorize the content. This makes it incredibly easy to skip errors or awkward wording, or to breeze past typos and boring descriptions.

That's why it's imperative in many writers' processes to read the story out loud. You need to *hear* the manuscript to fine-tune your style, address line editing issues, and fix those sneaky typos.

I recommend having your book read aloud at least once during the self-edit, but the more times, the better. You can read the manuscript out loud to yourself, or you can use an app like Edit Out Loud, which allows an AI to read the manuscript to you while you're driving, doing chores, or lounging.

Whichever method you choose, devote at least one pass-through to listening to the manuscript rather than reading it. It'll divulge far more errors than you'd likely anticipate.

MOVE ON

Sometimes writers fixate on an error they don't know how to rectify. I've been there myself. It can be really tempting to sit there for hours, obsessing over a problem you can't quite figure out . . .

Or you can highlight that bitch and move on.

I'm not telling you to ignore your issues. I'm encouraging you to save the tricky stuff for later. It's possible the answer will either come to you over time or you need to ask other writers for feedback. And remember, writers grow as they create. Hell, I *just* came up with a solution to my current work in progress that had been eluding me for a month.

Either way, there's no benefit in wasting precious hours mulling over the problem now. Make the most out of your time and focus on the issues you can fix right now in your current headspace. Don't worry about whatever's waiting; that's for future you to tackle, and I'm more than confident that future you is capable.

To help assist you during the self-editing phase, the next chapter is all about commonly made errors to pay attention to.

SUMMARY

THE DREADED SELF-EDIT

- Prior to sending it to anyone else, you're going to have to edit the manuscript yourself several times, to the point where you have polished your story as best as you can.

- Step-by-step guide to self-editing your novel:

- Go through your manuscript chapter by chapter and read everything. Do not edit at this step.
- Find your biggest issues. What are your most repeated phrases and words? Which characters aren't capturing your attention? Which scenes need to be rewritten or axed?
- Highlight, make bold, or mark the mistakes you find so future you can locate them with ease. The point of this step is to label mistakes so they're easier to find and fix during the self-edit.
- Leave comments and questions within the document if there are specific issues that require thought and strategy. This helps point your future self in the right direction while also silencing the internal overwhelm.
- Address inconsistencies. This is the first and only edit I recommend you make at this point. These are changes you've decided to make that affect the entirety of the novel. For

example, a character's name, the name of a setting, or the spelling of a fantasy word.

- List your most common mistakes. These are the errors that need the most work and education. This list will show you exactly where to hone your skills.
- Categorize your list into three sections: developmental issues, issues with prose, and all things related to grammar.
- Section your self-edit on a chapter-by-chapter basis to encourage focus.
- Listen to your story. When the content of your book is read out loud, mistakes and clunky sentences stand out.
- Save the tricky stuff for later. It's possible the answer will come to you over time, or you need to ask other writers for feedback.

CHAPTER 21
COMMON WRITING QUIRKS

THE MISTAKES YOU'RE PROBABLY, DEFINITELY GOING TO MAKE

YOU'VE BEEN MAKING a list of personal quirks in your writing, right? That will certainly help the editing process, but you're going to need a bit more insight than that. Sometimes writers make a buttload of mistakes they're blind to, mostly because they don't know it's a mistake to begin with. Thus, I'm breaking down some of the most common mistakes writers make while drafting their story. In the grand overwhelm of self-editing, you might've missed these boogers or didn't realize they were such a big deal. Diving deeper into your manuscript is why we're here, right?

These mistakes aren't universal, nor does this list cover all potential screw ups. Hell, if I were to list every mistake imaginable, that would be an encyclopedia in and of itself. But these bumps and bungles are particularly widespread, so it's a good idea to keep an eye out for them in your manuscript.

MISTAKES ON A STORY LEVEL

No structure

Even though I've hammered structure into your head so much throughout this book, it bears repeating. If you feel as though your story meanders, then you didn't follow the plot. Not only will this often make your story seem too short (because you skipped vital structural steps), but it usually results in buckets of filler.

Go through your story and make sure you've covered every key point necessary to qualify as a plot. If not, it's time to get back to planning. Reverse outlining—outlining after the draft has been written—exists for this very reason.

Filler

Many writers freak out when I say this, but I'm saying it anyway. *If the scene doesn't drive the plot forward, delete it.* That's not to say each scene needs an earth-shattering plot point, but they should all be relevant and necessary to the story.

Not sure if a scene is filler? Imagine you've removed it from the manuscript. If you can continue telling the story without issue, then it's filler.

But Jenna, it provides character development!

My darling writer, we covered this in Chapter 11. Your character should develop through the events of the plot. Part of the art of writing is interweaving the growth and complexity of your cast with the storyline itself. Filler does your manuscript no favors, which is why it needs to get the chop.

Not beginning where the story begins

As we discussed in Chapter 10, your first page needs to be engaging. No info dumps. No endless backstory. No boring descriptions of the weather. And don't even think about resorting to telling rather than showing at the start; that's a one-way ticket to a DNF (Did Not Finish).

If you're not sure how to start your book, here's a simple solution: Start at the beginning of the plot. Nine times out of ten, a story will include some type of problem that kicks off the inciting incident. Start your book with the problem. If the plot doesn't begin until several chapters into the book, trust me, no one's going to wait that long.

Info dumping

Look for scenes that drag. Maybe a scene is super important for your book, but it rambles on with dull exposition. Maybe there's too much explanation about your magical world, the history of the planet, or the bloodline of your leading character. All of this constitutes an info dump —paragraphs of facts that are boring to get through and mostly unnecessary to the story.

There's a difference between a long scene and a scene that drags. A long scene might be exciting and intense the whole way through. If that's the case, leave it alone. But a scene that drags is one that feels long no matter the length. It's a pain to slog through because it pauses the story—and the intrigue—for some useless blabbering.

Look for moments within scenes that don't benefit the story and give them the boot. This could be a couple lines of exposition-dumping dialogue. It could be a drawn-out description of every single leaf on a nearby tree. Locate each info dump, and cut it down to its most interesting, vital parts.

Realistic characterization

I'm not telling you to eliminate things like wizards and dragons, but your real-world content—relationships and dialogue, for example— needs to make logical sense. Your story may not be based in realism, but the characters within it should be believable enough for your readers to relate to them.

Your readers need to believe the protagonist and their love interest would realistically be attracted to each other. You can achieve this by creating chemistry and building the characters as complements to one another. Your readers need to believe your character would realistically say the things you've written into their dialogue. You do this by putting yourself in the character's position and giving them a human experience.

What you don't want is readers flipping through your pages, shaking their head while thinking, *People don't do this shit.*

The solution is simple. Go through your story and ask yourself, does this make sense? Not for the plot, but for the characters. Would this prince realistically fall in love with this soldier? Would this astronaut realistically make this speech? If the answer is no, it's time for a rewrite.

If you need a reminder on how to write realistic characters, review Chapter 4.

Sagging middle syndrome

You've got an awesome inciting incident and a badass climax. Unfortunately, the content that connects these two points sucks. Typically, this happens when the author doesn't outline their novel; if they did, it wasn't with enough detail or structure. Head back to Chapter 15 to review how to apply some professional tucking to that saggy middle. This is a very important mistake to correct because most readers won't be willing to power through a dull middle section, no matter how entertaining your climax promises to be.

All tell, no show

This is the most common story-level mistake I find among new writers. They tell everything and show absolutely nothing. It's much easier to tell than it is to show, which is why this mistake is so prevalent. A majority of the time, showing is the superior option.

If you're not quite sure how to differentiate show from tell, it's all in the description. Telling means to simply state an action, opinion, or fact to the reader. For example:

She had beautiful hair.

Showing, on the other hand, requires painting a picture, utilizing the five senses, and allowing readers to experience the story through their mind's eye. For example:

Onyx waves cascaded down her shoulders, reflecting the brilliant glow of the moonlight.

Okay, this example is a little cheesy, but it gets the point across. The first example is too simple, tells the reader how to feel, and doesn't evoke any emotion. The second example, however, creates a visual the reader can imagine while still portraying the overall message—this chick has some enviable hair!

Don't just recount the events of the story. Too much telling will destroy the ability of the reader to immerse themselves in the novel. It's not impactful to tell the reader, "They were best friends, and she loved him like a brother." Instead, write their playful banter and show their sibling-like bond through action and dialogue.

Telling certainly has its place in fiction, like when writing transitions or increasing the pace. But for situations that call for immersion and detail, showing is far more evocative. Locate places in your writing where you told the reader something that ought to be shown and make the switcheroo.

MISTAKES ON A PARAGRAPH AND SENTENCE LEVEL

Filter words

Filter words are probably the most common writing quirk in existence. I don't think I've met a writer who hasn't struggled with them at some point.

Filter words are words that filter the reader's experience through the main character's point of view. See, hear, think, realize, feel—these are all filter words. Sometimes they're unavoidable, but most of the time they're unnecessary. They serve little purpose other than distancing the reader from the story beats, which is the opposite of what you want.

Fortunately, filter words are very easy to eliminate.

For example, say you wrote the sentence, *I felt wind tousling my hair.*

Instead, you can simply write it as, *Wind tousled my hair.*

It appears I'm in a hairy mood this chapter. Just roll with it.

As you can see, it's the same sentiment with fewer words. Nixing the filter word creates a more immersive experience and allows readers to feel as though they're experiencing the action themselves.

When you go through your manuscript, pay attention to filter words, and see if you can cut them. Some filter words will get the greenlight, but most will require the axe.

Crutch words

Crutch words are words we have a habit of using repeatedly, even when there are other options available. You may think you don't have any crutch words, but that's because they're invisible to us. We usually don't realize we're repeating ourselves until someone else points it out. In my last manuscript, I used the word "scurry" so many times, one of my critique partners left crab gifs all over the document.

Because we don't notice our crutch words, this is a hard issue to dodge. Instead, ask your critique partner to be on the lookout for repetition. Another set of eyes can go a long way in revealing your crutch words so you can avoid them in the future. You can also run your manuscript through a program such as ProWritingAid.

Once your crutch words are on display, do a search through your manuscript and replace them with synonyms. After you've been made aware of them, it's much easier to avoid them in the future.

Echoes

While crutch words refer to overusing a word throughout the entirety of a manuscript, echoes refer to using the same word multiple times in close proximity. That doesn't mean this word is a crutch, but you've used it too much in a particular scene or on a particular page. Echoes should be avoided because they lead to a clunky reading experience.

There are going to be words that get a lot of use, like "the," "and," and various pronouns. I'm not talking about those words necessarily. Instead, I'm referring to words that are more noticeable when repeated. For example, did you write "purple" twice in the same paragraph? Have you referenced the balcony three times on one page? Does your fight scene use the word "stab" five times?

This is another quirk that can be hard to notice at first, which is why it's great to have critique partners read over your work or run your manuscript through ProWritingAid. It also helps to read your writing out loud. Upon hearing your writing, this type of repetition becomes way more obvious. If you're not keen on reading the story out loud to yourself, remember you can have an app like Edit Out Loud read the story to you.

Once your echoes are pointed out, see if they can be replaced with synonyms or removed entirely. After all, stab can easily become slice, jab, cut, skewer, or impale.

Adverbs

You've probably heard plenty of famous authors bemoan adverbs, but they aren't inherently evil. Every word serves a purpose, and adverbs are no different. But when authors begin overusing them, that's when adverbs really stink up the page.

Do a search through your manuscript of every verb and adverb combo. Is the adverb necessary? Most of the time, adverbs describe actions. But quite often, actions already describe themselves. No one needs to say, "I ran quickly," because the act of running is already quick.

Say you wrote, *She smiled happily.* The adverb "happily" is pointless because the definition of a smile is an amused expression. But if you wrote, *She smiled uncomfortably,* that makes more sense. The adverb "uncomfortably" showcases the fact that the action—a smile—isn't happening as the reader would expect.

What if the character is smiling widely? The adverb technically works, but that's only because you've chosen a weak verb for this action. What if the character was grinning instead? The definition of a grin is a wide smile. By using this more accurate verb, you've eliminated the need for the adverb altogether.

Commas

Punctuation is the bane of most writers' existence, and there is no worse punctuation foe than commas. Unfortunately, punctuation—*especially* commas—is a vital part of the writing process, seeing as they separate words and phrases. It's hard to create a polished, readable manuscript with zero knowledge of punctuation, which is why I encourage all writers to educate themselves thoroughly on the topic.

I hate to be the bearer of bad news (that's a lie), but punctuation errors stand out in the most obnoxious way. Even worse, comma rules are incredibly complex—too complex for a single chapter of a book, let alone a subsection. On the plus side, there are countless free tools available online boasting tons of education regarding commas. Additionally, software like ProWritingAid can point out your comma errors while also teaching you punctuation rules. If this is your area of weakness, I highly recommend taking advantage of these resources.

Homophones

Homophones are words that sound alike but are spelled differently and have different meanings. Obvious examples are "there," "their," and "they're," and "to," "two," and "too."

These little jerks sneak into manuscripts all the time, especially if you're not well versed in their definitions. Again, critique partners or writing software can help point these issues out, but if you want to ensure this problem is no longer one of your quirks, you need to learn the definitions of these words. For example, "there" is a place, "their" is ownership, and "they're" is short for *they are*. Drilling these definitions into your brain will make homophone phobia a thing of the past.

Dialogue tags

I don't care what your elementary school English teacher told you, "said" is *not* dead. Somewhere along the line, most writers—myself included—were encouraged to use colorful dialogue tags like exclaimed, queried, or ejaculated. If writing advice was a department store, I'd don my best Karen hairdo and demand to speak to the manager.

Here's the truth: Said is a great dialogue tag because it's invisible. Readers don't notice it unless it's used too often in close proximity, which makes the dialogue flow naturally and with minimal interruption.

But Jenna, I can't just use said a million times on a single page!

You shouldn't need a million dialogue tags on a single page, period. Dialogue tags exist to let readers know who is speaking. If readers can easily determine the speaker based on the number of people in the conversation, the surrounding narrative, or the dialogue itself, you don't need a tag whatsoever.

For the times you absolutely do need a tag, ask yourself, is the character's voice unusual right now? Is it a whisper, mumble, or shout? In those unique situations, you can use the applicable dialogue tags. However, said will most likely be your best bet.

Shifts in tense

You've already chosen a tense to write in at this point. However, many writers struggle with keeping that tense consistent. Shifting from past to present tense may look something like this:

He was so happy to see her. She looks amazing.

In this example, the verbs tell us everything we need to know. "Was" is past tense, whereas "looks" is present tense.

Part of correcting this issue is understanding what *isn't* a shift in tense. If you're writing your book in the past tense, dialogue and internal dialogue should still be written in the present tense. Just because the story itself happened years ago doesn't mean the characters are cognizant of that. For them, they're speaking in their version of now. An example of this would be, *She twirled across the stage and said, "I'm back, baby!"*

It's also important not to confuse present participles with shifts in tense. For example, the sentence, *She righted herself, breathing deeply*, is past tense, despite the word "breathing" being present tense. In this situation, "breathing" is a present participle, not a shift in tense.

If you need a refresher on tense, head back to Chapter 7.

Shifts in point of view

If your story is being told through the protagonist's perspective, it needs to remain in their point of view at all times. If your story is being told via multiple perspectives, then you need to stick with the point of view you're channeling in any given scene. Multiple perspectives are typically divided up by scene breaks or chapters. If you switch perspectives in the middle of a scene, that's called head hopping, and that's a big writerly no-no.

If you're writing in first person, this issue is much easier to avoid. But if you're a third person writer like myself, shifts in point of view are a lot harder to catch. That doesn't mean it's unavoidable. Maintaining the correct perspective is all about honoring what your character knows to be true and sticking with it.

In *The Savior's Champion*, I wrote from the perspective of Tobias, which means the narration could only comment on what Tobias sees, experiences, and knows. Tobias is aware the queen of his realm is magical, but he doesn't know how her magic works. That means if the narration were to suddenly slip into an explanation of her powers, that would be considered a shift in point of view. Tobias hasn't a clue how the Queen's magic works, which means the narration has left his perspective completely.

If you feel as though your perspective is becoming blurry, ask yourself, does my character have any idea about whatever it is I'm currently writing? If the answer is no, it's time to rewrite.

UNDERWRITERS VERSUS OVERWRITERS

As you're editing, you might notice that you fall into one of two camps: underwriter or overwriter.

An underwriter is someone whose first draft is far too simple and lacks depth. We often refer to these drafts as bare bones, as they require a lot more meat to make them feel whole. Inversely, an overwriter is someone who can't seem to shut up. Their writing rambles, repeats itself, and meanders into filler territory.

If you can relate to either of these points, no need to hang your head in shame. No one's first draft is perfect, remember? We all fall into one of these camps. These issues are precisely why editing exists in the first place.

Based on which label fits you best, you may need to focus on different things during the self-editing process. For example, underwriters will likely want to focus on structure, beefing up their characterization, and showing as opposed to telling. Pay special attention to that last point when it comes to character relationships, setting the scene, descriptions, and subplots.

Overwriters tend to put a greater focus on tightening info dumps, erasing filler, and nixing filter words and adverbs. If you're an overwriter, it's great to implement a *trimming* phase during self-editing; go through your manuscript and trim any words, sentences, or scenes that do not serve the overall plot.

Here's some good news: Once you determine if you have an under- or overwriting inclination, it becomes much easier to avoid it in the future. The more I write, the less I see my bad habits popping up, which means my first drafts become cleaner and cleaner as I grow. I wouldn't be surprised if you experienced the same metamorphosis over time.

Now that the self-edit is over, you may think it's time to dive into the professional edit. We're not quite there yet. First, it's time to determine your genre and category.

SUMMARY
COMMON WRITING QUIRKS

- Story-level mistakes you should look for while self-editing:

- *No structure.* Make sure you've covered every key point necessary for the plot. If not, go back to the planning stage.
- *Filler.* If the scene doesn't drive the plot forward, delete it. Every scene should be relevant.
- *Not beginning where the story begins.* Start at the beginning of the plot. Most stories will include some type of problem that kicks off the inciting incident.
- *Info dumping.* Look for scenes that drag and cut them.
- *Realistic characterization.* Make sure your characters, character relationships, and dialogue make logical sense to the reader.
- *Sagging middle syndrome.* This happens when the author doesn't outline their novel; if they did, it wasn't with enough detail or structure.
- *All tell, no show.* Showing is much more evocative than telling. It creates clearer pictures for the reader so they can see and feel what the character is experiencing.

- Paragraph and sentence level mistakes you should look for while self-editing:

- *Filter Words*. Filter words are words that filter the reader's experience through the main character's experience. Sometimes filter words are unavoidable, but most of the time, they aren't necessary.
- *Crutch words*. Crutch words are words we have a habit of using repeatedly, even when there are better options. Have someone else read your work and mark your crutch words or use a grammar checker like ProWritingAid.
- *Echoes*. Echoes refer to the use of the same word multiple times in close proximity. It's good to have critique partners read over your work or run your manuscript through a writing software.
- *Adverbs*. An adverb typically describes an action. They're usually unnecessary since many actions already describe themselves.
- *Commas*. Educate yourself on correct usages *and* hire an editor.
- *Homophones*. Homophones are words that sound alike but are spelled differently and have different meanings. Understand what these words mean so you know when to use them.
- *Dialogue tags*. Dialogue tags let the reader know who is speaking. If the reader can easily tell who is speaking based on the number of people in the conversation or the narrative surrounding the dialogue, you don't need a dialogue tag.
- *Shifts in tense*. Your verbs will tell you if and when you've shifted from the appropriate tense.
- *Shifts in point of view*. If the scene is supposed to be told from one character's perspective, you do not want to shift the point of view.

- Underwriters and overwriters:

- An underwriter is someone whose story is way too simple and lacks depth. Focus on structure, making your characters realistic, and showing as opposed to telling.

- An overwriter is someone who can't seem to stop writing. Focus on eliminating info dumps, filler, filter words, and adverbs.

CHAPTER 22
GENRES AND CATEGORIES

PUTTING YOUR BOOK INTO
A BOX

AMID THE SELF-EDITING PHASE, you're going to want to nail down your manuscript's genre and category. You probably already had an idea of it at the start of the writing process, but stories evolve as we write. Now's the time to determine the boxes your story really fits into.

Okay, maybe artists don't like feeling labeled, but this step can't be skipped. Genres and categories are some of your most important marketing tools because they ensure the ideal audience reads your book.

In its simplest terms, **genre** is a category of literature based on the style and content of the story in question. Think about the applicable setting, characters, tropes, creatures, and conflicts. All these nuances go into defining your novel's genre.

You probably know quite a few genres off the top of your head. If not, it's time to do a whole lot of research because this is going to be a bumpy journey without the appropriate know-how. For the sake of easing you in, here are some of the most popular fiction genres you can expect to find:

Romance is the most popular fiction genre by a landslide, covering the romantic relationship between two or more characters and ending in a happily ever after (HEA) or happy for now (HFN).

Mystery is another very popular genre that follows a crime—most often a murder—from the moment it happens to the point when it's inevitably solved.

Horror is a genre designed to scare its audience or create feelings of disgust and dread.

Fantasy revolves around adventure, either involving magic, fictional worlds, or both. Fantasy is often influenced by folklore and mythology.

Science fiction, or sci-fi, takes place in the future or involves futuristic elements and technology. Space travel and aliens are common in sci-fi, but not required.

Do any of these sound familiar to you? If not, I can only assume you've been locked away for centuries. I'd love to say the research ends here, but there are tons of other genres out there, which can make labeling your novel pretty damned confusing.

But Jenna, why the hell do so many genres exist?

Subgenres, my darling writer. Many genres are very broad and encapsulate thousands, if not millions, of books. For example, fantasy covers adventure, fictional worlds, and magic. This describes everything from *A Song of Ice and Fire* to *My Little Pony*. The subgenres, or smaller categories within a genre, help to narrow the content down even further.

Does your fantasy novel include long quests with robust world-building? Then it sounds like you're writing an epic fantasy novel. Is it littered with violence and an overarching theme of death? That, my friend, is a dark fantasy novel. Does it take place in our world, on good ole planet Earth? You've got yourself a contemporary fantasy novel.

Pull up the Google machine and dig deep. Familiarize yourself with the genres and subgenres best suited for your story and get to know their rules and terminology. This will allow you to create a list of possibilities you can narrow down.

That's the hard part: taking your list of ten or more possible genres and limiting it to one or two. As writers, it's easy for us to assume every teeny tiny nuance in our book is important. And they are important—just not when it comes to pinning down your genre. For this, you're going to break your book down to its most vital parts by asking yourself a few questions.

What is the plot?

What is the meat of your story? We're not talking about subplots here, as they don't affect the genre of your novel. I repeat, *ignore your subplots*. If your book is all about an intergalactic war, but along the way a space soldier and alien find love, that's wonderful, but it doesn't make your book a romance. Put that genre down and walk away slowly.

Some genres are frequently plot driven. Action-adventure novels revolve around—you guessed it—action and adventure. You'll often find quite a bit of adventure in fantasy and sci-fi stories. Other genres are more character driven. If you've written a romance, your story will follow the blooming connection between your adorable love birds.

Zero in on the main plot of your story. It should be easy to do, as you're the one who wrote it. Remove the subplots and fluff from the equation, and allow that singular, primary concept to guide your genre selection.

Where and when does the book take place?

If your book takes place on Mars in the year 3015, we can safely assume you've written some brand of sci-fi. If your book takes place in a world overrun with unicorns, you should be well aware it's fantasy. If your book takes place in 1492, when that bastard Columbus sailed the ocean blue, we can set our sights on historical fiction. And if your book takes place in the here and now, we're working with something contemporary.

Are there ghosts? Monsters? Centaurs?

If you've got any creatures that go bump in the night, you may have written a horror story. If you have demons or ghosts, then you most likely have a paranormal novel. What about fairies, dragons, and elves, oh my! That right there is a fantasy book.

What are the rules?

Writers are rule breakers by nature, but this ain't the time for it. If you classify your story as a particular genre, you better be damned sure it follows the appropriate rules.

For example, romance novels are required to end with a happily ever after (HEA) or a happy for now (HFN). Without this, it can't be labeled a romance. That means no sad or tragic endings. You might be ready to argue, citing stories like *Romeo and Juliet*—except *Romeo and Juliet* is a tragedy, not a romance. Just because a story follows a couple in love doesn't necessarily mean it's a romance.

Which brings us full circle. Learn the rules and follow them. Want to write about two star-crossed lovers who die at the end? Have at it. Just label it the correct genre.

Maybe you've gone through all these steps and you're still feeling flustered.

But Jenna, my story fits more than one genre!

That's fine too.

It's common for books to be labeled under more than one genre. *The Savior's Champion* is a dark fantasy romance, as the plot revolves around a romantic relationship within a deadly, magical world. If your book fits two genres—*maybe* three—combine them.

Sci-fi fantasy. Historical romance. Erotic thriller. These are all popular multi-genre pairings, and they certainly don't deter readers. The key is to be honest with yourself when choosing these qualifiers. Remember, we're not taking every single subplot into consideration. Just because your story is complex and unique doesn't mean you get to tack on twelve genres and call yourself special. Well, you can if you want to, but no one will end up reading your book.

All right, do you have your genre figured out? Great. But we're not done yet. It's time to talk about categories.

Categories reflect the age of the target audience of your novel. You are letting the masses know, I wrote this book for *this* specific type of human being.

The good news: Unlike the infinite examples of genre, there are only a handful of categories for novels.

The bad news: Writers tend to have more trouble choosing their category than their genre.

If there are only a few categories to choose from, why is the choice so difficult? Blame the publishing industry. While the qualifiers for each age category are clear, publishing houses are famous for fudging the rules and blurring the lines for the sake of profitability. If a particular category is on trend, publishers may take books from another category and promote them similarly as if they belong. Not sure what I mean? Have you seen smutty novels marketed for thirteen-year-olds? Yeah. That.

If you're as confused as most writers, allow me to break down the various categories in detail.

Let's start with **adult** fiction, also known as the standard, or "trade" category of fiction. People hear "adult" and tend to think it means pornographic, but that's not what this title refers to. In the world of publishing, all books are assumed adult until proven otherwise because adult is the oldest category. Before young adult or middle grade existed, adult novels reigned supreme.

Since it's the "standard" category, you'll rarely see books defined as "adult fantasy" or "adult historical fiction." If there's no categorical qualifier listed, you can assume the story is adult.

An adult novel simply means the story was written for an adult readership. The characters are quite often adults as well—ages twenty and older—though there can be exceptions. *A Song of Ice and Fire* has a few thirteen-year-old protagonists thrown into the mix, but no one would argue the book was written for middle schoolers. Similarly, *The Bad Seed* revolves around a child, but this psychological horror was written to haunt adults.

Sex, swearing, or violence aren't required in adult novels. Plenty of trade fiction is wholesome and squeaky clean. It also doesn't mean teens can't read these books. It just means teenage or childhood interests weren't taken into consideration upon writing these stories, as they're not the target audience.

Now that the trade category is out of the way, let's take a look at niche categories: middle grade, young adult, and new adult. These categories are considered niche because they're written for a very small segment of the population, whereas adult novels cover decades of age groups.

Middle grade novels are written for middle schoolers. The targeted readership is ages 8 to 12, and the stories often feature characters ages 8 to 12. Books like *Percy Jackson and the Lightning Thief* and *Ella Enchanted* fall under this category.

Middle grade stories are typically written in a simple, easy-to-digest style for their younger audience and cover themes like friendship, adventure, and self-confidence. There may be battles and fight scenes, but no gruesome violence, as well as no swearing or sexual content. Remember, the kids reading these books are just that—kids! The most salacious content you'll find in a middle grade book is a sweet kiss on the lips.

Young adult novels are written for teenagers. Readers are typically aged 12 to 18, and the characters in these books will usually also be 12 to 18 years old—maybe 19 on the rare occasion. If you're familiar with *The Hunger Games* and *The Outsiders*, then you're familiar with young adult fiction.

Young adult books are often faster paced and voicy, reflective of the main character's personality and beliefs. You'll find themes that appeal to teenagers, like self-discovery, coming of age, finding your voice, and young love. Swearing, sex, and violence can make an appearance in young adult books, but be cautious. Remember, 12-year-olds read these books too. That means the curse words may be in shorter supply, the sex isn't graphic, and the violence doesn't bleed into pure gore.

Some people hear these rules and take it to the extreme. Remember *The Hunger Games*? That's a young adult novel about child murder. Give it a read and see how the author handled the topic. It's certainly violent, but not too explicit. Countless young adult novels feature sex without diving into erotica territory. Words like cock and clit aren't utilized. Instead, readers are given an emotional experience as the characters explore each other's bodies.

New adult is the niche category that screws up writers the most. To this day, writers struggle to define it, so bear with me as I do my best.

New adult novels are written for college-aged readers, usually between the ages of 18 and 25. As a result, the characters are often between 18 and 25 years old. Books like *Losing It* and *All Lined Up* by Cora Carmack are considered new adult.

You may already be able to tell why new adult is such a confusing category—it overlaps the adult category. Adult fiction already covers characters ages 20 and up and can essentially follow any story or themes the author desires. So, why then does new adult exist in the first place?

That comes down to marketing. For a couple decades, young adult fiction became the most desired category among readers, while adult fiction fell into the background. A lot of young adult readers assumed adult fiction was stuffy and boring, not realizing the category covered a broad range of work. Thus, the new adult category was created so traditional publishers could promote more adult fiction to its adult readers of the young adult category. New adult was labeled as the middle ground between the two categories.

New adult books tend to feature themes of embarking into adulthood, like going off to college or getting your first job. They can also cover the exploration of love and sexuality. But as the years have gone by, more and more books are being called new adult simply because they appeal to both an adult and teenaged audience.

Ultimately, if your book features characters ages 20 to 25, you can likely label it as either new adult or adult. That's up to you and your marketing path. While I label *The Savior's Champion* as adult, seeing as it lacks any new adult themes, it could also be seen as new adult due to the age of the main characters.

That said, due to its recent creation and particular niche-ness, new adult is not widely considered an official category. You won't find a new adult section in a bookstore or on Amazon. As of publishing this book, it's a term mostly used for marketing purposes and little else.

Oof. That was tricky, huh? I hope you have an idea of your genre and category because we're switching gears to one of the most exciting parts of the writing process: titling your book.

SUMMARY
GENRES AND CATEGORIES

- Genre is defined as a category of literature based on style and content.

- Some prominent genres include:

  - Romance
  - Mystery
  - Horror
  - Fantasy
  - Science fiction

- Subgenres exist to further specify niches within a genre. For example, contemporary fantasy is fantasy that takes place in our modern world.

- To figure out your genre ask yourself:

  - What is the plot of the main story?
  - Where and when does the book take place?
  - Are there ghosts? Monsters? Centaurs?
  - What are the rules of the genre?

- If your book fits into two or three genres, it can be considered a multi-genre book, e.g., dark fantasy romance.

- Categories reflect the age of your target audience.

- Adult: the "standard" category for fiction. All books are assumed to be adult until proven otherwise.
- Middle grade: the category written for middle schoolers, featuring characters in the 8- to 12-year-old range. Books include themes of friendship or adventure and feature no adult content, such as swearing and sex.
- Young adult: the category written for teenagers, featuring characters ages 12 to 18. Books include themes of self-discovery and coming of age and feature adult content cautiously. Sex scenes and violence can be included but shouldn't be excessive.
- New adult: the category written for college-aged readers, featuring characters ages 18 to 25. New adult heavily overlaps the adult category, as it was created to help market adult content to adult readers of young adult fiction.

CHAPTER 23
TITLING YOUR NOVEL
WHAT'S IN A NAME? LITERALLY EVERYTHING

TITLING a book is one of those experiences that's either a piece of cake or a nightmare. There are only two options: You know your title instantly, or you're slamming your head against a wall for months. If you're in the latter position, this chapter's for you, but even if you have your title figured out, I encourage you to read along. There are a lot of points to take into consideration when choosing a title, and your choice can make the difference between sales and a flop.

Let's break down all the things you need to consider to select a marketable book title.

Genre relevance

Similar to your genre, your title is a marketing tool designed to attract the right audience. That means your title needs to both fit your genre and create intrigue. No, you don't have to communicate the entire plot of your novel in the title alone. That would be nearly impossible to do unless you plan to create a title that's a paragraph long (please don't do that). But certain words and phrases are common within particular genres and send appropriate signals to the right audience.

If a title has the word "king" or "queen" in it, readers might assume it's a fantasy. If a title has the word "stalker" in it, they'll probably assume it's a thriller or mystery. "Invasion" lends itself best to sci-fi, but it could also fit dystopia or war fiction. Be aware of the words you're choosing, the messages they convey, and whether they fit your genre(s).

Trends

Look at bestselling books in your genre and category. What sort of trends are you seeing?

As of this book's publication, one of the most obvious title trends is within the young adult category. Every other young adult book features this title format: *The/A [blank] of/so [blank] and [blank]*.

A Song of Wraiths and Ruin. A Curse So Dark and Lonely. The Ballad of Songbirds and Snakes.

See what I mean?

That's not to say you should copy what others are doing or hop aboard the train just because it's trending. It's great to stand out! But familiarizing yourself with the trends helps you find your place among them. I personally don't recommend bold replication, because then your work becomes interchangeable with every other book on the shelf. But I think it's great to analyze trends to see how you can find your own place within them—a way to be modern and current, but still your own unique voice.

SEO

Search Engine Optimization, or SEO, refers to calculated decisions that give your book visibility in search results. There are a million ways to use SEO when releasing a book, and one of those ways is to consider the title.

There are platforms that will show you commonly searched words that often appear in specific genre titles. Through the website K-lytics, you can download a report all about your genre, including appropriate keywords, cover art trends, and search history. It'll also list the most frequent words used in the top one hundred bestselling book titles within that genre. When I pulled up a K-lytics dark fantasy report, some of the most popular words were "queen," "mage," "blood," and "master."

This may help you narrow down your title options by showing you which words get better search results from your target audience.

What is your book about?

Surely you considered this, right? Maybe? Unfortunately, a lot of writers are so busy searching the minute details, they overlook the answer staring them right in the face.

Is your book about a fallen soldier? Then maybe you should call it *Fallen Soldier*.

Is your book about a twenty-year war? Maybe it should be called *Twenty Years of War*.

The Savior's Champion is called *The Savior's Champion* because it's literally about a man competing to become—wait for it—the savior's champion.

If it ain't broke, don't fix it. Keep it simple, stupid. The simplest solution is always the best. Another age-old platitude. Sometimes it's as easy as stating the plot in its most basic form.

Symbols and themes

What are some recurring symbols, themes, and imagery that pop up in your story? Sometimes these concepts are important enough to be reflected in the title. If you're writing a book involving elemental magic, then earth, air, fire, and water are likely recurring symbols. If you're writing a werewolf book, words like wolves, pack, moonlight, and howling are worth considering.

Make a list of these words and combine them into coherent phrases. Which ones speak to you? What captures the essence of this story? This process is a huge winner when it comes to titling your book. I've seen more writers get results from it than not. At the very least, it'll give you a variety of options to choose from, and that's a great place to find yourself.

Quotations

Sometimes the title of your novel will reveal itself in the dialogue or narrative you've written. Works like *A Clockwork Orange* are titled based on specific lines featured in the books themselves. These titles are a bit more nuanced—after all, you don't read "A Clockwork Orange" and immediately think dystopia—but they're fun for readers. It's exciting to read a book and suddenly stumble across the title drop.

This method won't work for everyone, but it's worth exploring if you have meaningful, thematic quotes within your story.

Title erasure

Just like there are ways to improve your search results, there are also plenty of ways to screw them up.

An example of this is one-word titles. I'm sure you can think of a few one-word titles that have made it big: *Cinder. Circe. You.* I'm not saying you can never, *ever* follow this format. But you must know that, unless the author or the book itself is quite famous, one-word titles are hard to search for online.

Say you've decided to title your book *Hazard*. That's a pretty flashy title, and I myself am a fan of it. But when people google *Hazard*, they're going to get a million results that have nothing to do with your book—the definition of the word, various biohazards throughout history, even people with the surname Hazard. You may decide to risk it and power through but do so knowing the uphill climb you're about to face.

Another search hurdle is choosing words that have a strong link to something else quite popular. If you decide to write a fantasy novel titled *The Power of Elsa*, people are immediately going to assume it's related to Disney's *Frozen*—or at the very least that it's *Frozen* fanfiction.

But the worst way to damn your book is to give it a title that already exists in mainstream media. Is your title of choice the name of another book, movie, TV show, video game, or comic book? If that other work is unknown and obscure, you might be in the clear. But if it's even mildly popular, whenever people google that title, they're going to find that other piece of media, not yours. It's time to look for something new.

Ask the audience

After you've gone through these points, there's a good chance you'll have a short list of possibilities. This is when it helps to simply *ask*. Talk to other readers and writers. Show them your titles and ask them what they like best.

Better yet, ask them *why* they like the title they've chosen. This can be super revealing, as it'll give you direct access to your audience's mentality. You're very close to your book, which means you're looking at your options from a unique perspective. Readers have a completely different view of your story, so their opinions may surprise you. Whether you're asking your critique partners or your direct audience, it's always a good idea to pool opinions before settling on a title.

See? That wasn't so bad. Now let's get our manuscript polished with a little help from our friends.

SUMMARY
TITLING YOUR NOVEL

- When choosing a marketable title, consider:

- *Genre relevance.* Your title needs to fit your genre by choosing words that lend themselves to the content.
- *Trends.* Look at bestselling books in your genre and category. What sort of trends are you seeing?
- *SEO.* Make your book pop up in search results. There are platforms, like K-lytics, that show commonly searched words that often appear in the titles of specific genres.
- *What is your book about?* Sometimes the most obvious title is the best title.
- *Symbols and themes.* What are some recurring symbols, themes, and imagery that pop up in your story? Sometimes these things are important enough to be reflected in the title.
- *Quotations.* Sometimes the title of your novel will reveal itself in the dialogue or narrative you've written.
- *Title erasure.* Avoid practices that make your title a marketing hindrance. For example, duplicating a title with a strong link to another piece of popular media will decrease your book's exposure.

- *Ask the audience.* Show other readers and writers your title options and ask them what they like best.

CHAPTER 24

CRITIQUE PARTNERS, BETA READERS, AND SENSITIVITY READERS
A LITTLE HELP FROM MY FRIENDS

I MENTIONED EARLY on that this book would cover the writing process from start to finish in sequential order, with a wee bit of wiggle room here and there. Well, this is one of those wiggly parts. Recruiting help from others can happen at various stages during the writing process; in fact, I encourage you to do just that. But I'm listing this chapter here, toward the end, for a specific reason.

We're about to cover the three primary helpers you'll need during the writing process: critique partners, beta readers, and sensitivity readers. Two of those three helpers, in my opinion, should be recruited at this very step in your writing process—after the self-edit, genre and category selection, and titling, but before the professional edit. We'll cover the intricacies of each of these helpers and why their timing matters now.

CRITIQUE PARTNERS

A critique partner, or CP, is a fellow writer who reviews your manuscript. They're given permission to leave trackable edits and comments within the document itself as well as a written assessment or evaluation at the end of the manuscript or section. You can advise them to pay attention to specific issues, like grammar or world-building, or you can allow them to point out any strengths or weaknesses they find.

But Jenna, isn't that what an editor is for?

This is an easy assumption to make if you've never experienced a professional edit. A critique, while helpful, is significantly less in-depth than an edit. For starters, editors are highly trained in their craft, whereas critique partners are usually writers with their own personal strong suits and faults. There's going to be an inevitable difference in skill level. Editors point out every minute issue they can find, provide thorough explanations backed by education, answer your questions, and troubleshoot your tricky spots. Certain editors, like copyeditors, will fix every mistake they find in your manuscript. A critique partner won't go to those lengths, but that's no excuse to skip this step.

When it comes to critique partners, you have a couple options. The first option is to pay for a professional critique, typically from an experienced writer or an editor offering smaller, inexpensive services. This is a great choice for anyone who'd like some direction regarding their writing but doesn't have time to return the favor.

Which brings us to the second option: Recruit from within the writing community. Create an arrangement with a fellow writer to swap manuscripts. They critique your writing, and you critique theirs. This is a very common practice, and many writers have multiple critique partners to suit their needs. I usually have about two or three for any given manuscript.

If this option sounds like a winner, what should you look for in a critique partner?

They should be at a similar skill level as you

You were hoping they'd be a way more accomplished writer than you are, weren't you? But if that were the case, how would this arrangement benefit them? Remember, you chose to *swap* manuscripts, which means this has to be equally advantageous for them.

If possible, look for writers at your level with skills that complement or balance out yours. If your prose is stellar, find a critique partner who's an amazing storyteller. If you're a character writer, find a world-builder.

They should enjoy the genre you're writing

Otherwise critiquing is going be a real pain in the ass. Plus, if they don't read your genre, how exactly are they supposed to help you? Their lack of expertise will make their critiques mostly useless.

You should probably get along with them

Each one of my critique partners is a close friend. This isn't a mandatory part of the process, but it certainly helps. You're going to be in frequent communication with this person for extended periods of time. It's important you like one another, communicate well, and understand each other. If you absolutely loathe this person, or barely even know them, this arrangement is going to be arduous.

You have the same expectations

Raise your hand if you've ever waited a full year for critique notes. It happens to the best of us, which is why clear communication is a must. Discuss the timeframe for your critique and what you expect out of it. Make sure you're on the same page to avoid any confusion. And remember, if someone can't hold up their end of the agreement, that's fine. You are well within your rights to part ways on good terms.

They offer more than compliments

This person is reading an unpublished draft of your manuscript. There's absolutely no way it's perfect. Compliments are wonderful, and it's helpful for your critique partner to let you know what they're enjoying in your story. But if that's all this exchange was about, it wouldn't be called a critique. If a critique partner is solely stroking your ego, they're either not skilled enough to locate errors, or they're too kind to deliver bad news.

They're not a dick

It's important to have a thick skin whenever you're receiving feedback, but if someone's mocking you, it's time to give them the boot. Just because they're not kissing ass doesn't mean they have to *be* an ass. There's a difference between critiquing and heckling. Critiques are rooted in thoughtful analysis, whereas heckling is purely cruelty.

Say I'm critiquing a chapter that's painfully dull. I could say just that, but how is it helpful? Instead, I could tell them the scene reads slowly due to the lengthy exposition. This feedback portrays the same message but with actionable detail and without the callousness.

Now that you know what to look for in a critique partner, when should you start looking? Honestly, that's a judgment call. I know writers who recruit critique partners to read their outlines. I usually have my critique partners look over my first few drafts. I know other writers who aren't comfortable with critiques until after the self-edit. Fly free and do what feels right to you. So long as you're enlisting critiques before the professional edit, you should be fine.

BETA READERS

A beta reader is a non-professional reader who reads through your manuscript with the intention of helping you improve your work. Their job is to give you a look into your future readership's perspective. What did they enjoy in your story? What did they dislike? Did they like your main character? Were they confused or overwhelmed?

Like critique partners, beta readers are usually volunteers recruited to help you finetune your story, but that's where the similarities end. While critique partners are fellow writers, beta readers are just that—readers. Sure, they *can* be writers, but it's not a requirement. They also don't leave edits or comments in the manuscript itself unless you've created a unique arrangement with them.

So, how does the beta reading process work? Based on their wants and needs, writers will send their beta readers several chapters at a time—I've found five chapters at once works best for me, but your process may be different. I do not recommend sending the entire manuscript at once, because your betas will likely forget details from the beginning and middle by the time they reach the end.

Once the beta has finished their section, they can either send the writer their overall thoughts and feelings, or the writer can provide a questionnaire seeking specific information. I recommend the latter so you can get a thorough look at your manuscript.

If you choose to send a questionnaire, here are some important questions to ask:

- What was your favorite scene and why?
- Were any parts confusing? Which ones, and how so?
- Were there any parts you didn't like? Which ones, and why?
- Are you eager to continue reading more? Why or why not?
- Do you have any predictions? If so, what are they?

You'll notice these questions include a "why?" and require elaboration. That's important! It's not enough to know a beta reader hated your chapters; you need to know why that was the case so you can make the appropriate changes.

I also encourage you to ask about every character and every scene within that section. I know—it sounds like a lot. But this will be crucial to not only determining whether your characters are likeable, but whether your content is being interpreted as you intended. Your beta readers may claim to love the section and find zero fault with it, but upon further prying, you learn they adore the villain when they're supposed to hate them, or they found the fight scene hilarious when it was supposed to be thrilling. That is why we ask about each character and scene. Just because a beta reader enjoyed your work doesn't mean they understood it, and that's feedback you need to hear.

It's also important to ask your betas about their theories and predictions, especially if your story includes any surprises, plot twists, or whodunnits. It's also not a bad idea to ask your betas for some kind of number rating out of 5 or 10. This question isn't imperative, but it might give you an idea of how much your story needs to improve.

Once the questionnaire is complete, the reader will receive the next group of chapters. This process continues until either the book is complete, or the beta reader asks to be removed from the process— which is feedback in itself.

When it comes to enlisting beta readers, the criteria are much less intense than they are for critique partners. Most importantly, your beta readers should be reflective of your target audience; if you're writing fantasy, they should be fantasy readers. Be sure to enlist a diverse pool of betas (different races, genders, etc.) to give you a well-rounded view of how your book is coming across from multiple perspectives.

You also want betas who give thorough feedback. Three-word answers do you no favors. Find beta readers who love to ramble! But most importantly, find beta readers who are *reliable*. The process can take a while, so make sure these people are in it for the long haul. Don't hound or bully them—they're volunteers, after all—but if you're waiting over a month for feedback, it's time to look elsewhere.

After the self-edit but before the professional edit is the sweet spot for beta readers because your manuscript is as clean as you can possibly make it on your own, which means it'll be an easier read for your betas. Enlisting betas after the professional edit would be a waste of both time and money. You'll inevitably have to rewrite entire sections and pay for another editor to review it all over again.

SENSITIVITY READERS

A lot of writers are unclear regarding the role of sensitivity readers. They assume it's their job to make the story clean-cut and inoffensive. While wholesome literature does exist, media is often designed to shock, horrify, and fascinate, and that means we're all bound to offend a reader or two along the way. Sensitivity readers are not here to turn your thriller into a children's book, but they can potentially turn a flop into a gem.

A sensitivity reader is a hired professional who looks through your manuscript for cultural inaccuracies, insensitive language, and misrepresentation regarding race, religion, disability, sexual orientation, or other topics. Simply put, it's their job to let you know if you've accidentally written something racist, sexist, homophobic, ableist, or bigoted in some other fashion. They help you create a more inclusive and accurate portrayal of your characters and world, especially if you're writing about a marginalized group you don't personally belong to.

I know what you're thinking: This doesn't pertain to me. I'm "woke." But we all make mistakes, we all have subconscious biases, and we all have our own areas of ignorance. A sensitivity reader isn't hired to berate you; after all, if you hired them, it means you care about this topic. Instead, they'll highlight sections of your story that aren't appropriate and explain to you why that is. Not only will this help you create a better novel, but you can avoid making these mistakes in the future.

Sensitivity readers usually have an area of expertise, such as trauma, racism, LGBTQIA+ characters, or various physical disabilities. They're often a member of said marginalized group or have undergone significant education regarding the topic at hand. Make sure the sensitivity reader you recruit is knowledgeable about whatever issues pertain to your story. I've listed my personal sensitivity readers in the resource section.

So, how does the process work? It's pretty similar to the critique or editing processes. You send them your manuscript, and they leave comments throughout the document, pointing out triggering or insensitive content. They will often write out an assessment at the end of their review.

Like with beta readers, I recommend hiring a sensitivity reader after the self-edit but before the professional edit. Not all manuscripts require a sensitivity reader, but if you're on the fence about whether you need one, you probably do.

Wasn't that fun? I love sharing my writing journey with friends. In the next chapter, we're taking things up a notch and sending our manuscript to the pros.

SUMMARY

CRITIQUE PARTNERS, BETA READERS, AND SENSITIVITY READERS

- Critique partners: a fellow writer who reviews your manuscript.

- A critique, also known as an assessment, is an evaluation of your work in progress.

- What to look for in a critique partner:

  - They should be at a similar skill level as you.
  - They should enjoy the genre you're writing.
  - You should get along with them.
  - You should have the same expectations.
  - They should offer more than compliments.
  - They shouldn't be a dick.

- Beta readers: a non-professional reader who reads through your story with the intention of helping you improve your work.

- The writer will either send their betas the whole book or a chunk of chapters, e.g., five chapters at a time.

- Once the beta has finished their section, the writer interviews them about their experience. Typically, you want to ask them opinion-based questions like:

- What was your favorite scene and why?
- Were any parts confusing? Which ones, and how so?
- Were there any parts you didn't like? Which ones, and why?
- Are you eager to continue reading more? Why or why not?
- Do you have any predictions? If so, what are they?

- You should also ask them about their impressions of every character and scene. You want to figure out if your story is entertaining and easy to follow or if it's too predictable or complicated. If readers aren't enjoying your story, why is that?

- What should you look for in a beta reader?

- They should enjoy the genre you're writing.
- They should reflect your target audience.
- They should give thorough feedback.
- They should be reliable.

- Sensitivity readers: a professional hired to read a manuscript and look for sensitivity issues like cultural inaccuracies or misrepresentation regarding race, religion, disability, sexual orientation, etc.

- The sensitivity reader is typically a member of said marginalized group.

- When seeking a sensitivity reader, they should specialize in the particular content relevant to your novel.

CHAPTER 25
THE PROFESSIONAL EDIT
YES, IT'S MANDATORY

THE PROFESSIONAL EDIT is one of the most important parts of the writing process. You've put so much hard work into your book baby, and now it's time to ship it off to skilled hands so they can rip it to shreds.

Yes, the professional edit can be painful, but it's necessary. Editors aren't hired to find a typo here and there. It's their job to refine your story from its plot to its prose. They're trained to have a keen eye for plot holes, inconsistencies, sentence structure, character development, and those pesky comma errors you never learned to correct. This process, while dreaded, polishes your manuscript for the masses. Without it, your book is pretty much doomed.

What type of editor should you hire? You're probably going to need more than one. There are four steps in the editing process, and the magnitude of each step will depend on your manuscript's strengths and weaknesses. But you'll likely need to go through each one of these edits, and you'll need to do so in the proper order.

TYPES OF PROFESSIONAL EDITS

Developmental edit

Developmental edits are the big picture edits. This type of editor focuses on plot, characterization, pacing, tone, and other larger facets of your overall story. It's helpful if they're proficient in your genre, as they'll also consider tropes, cliches, and reader expectations.

Line edit

The line edit sounds exactly like it is. An editor looks at the line-level of your book, including style and readability. This may cover word choice and sentence structure as well as improving the flow of your sentences. It can also cover repetition, paragraph formatting, and language.

Copyedit

A copyedit focuses on the mechanics of your writing, such as grammar, spelling, and punctuation. This is more of a technical edit that will smooth out the small wrinkles in your prose.

Proofread

The proofread is the final line of defense. Proofreaders look for any small errors that have slipped through the cracks: typos, misplaced punctuation, or formatting mix-ups that have gone unnoticed.

It's important to note that a proofread doesn't replace an editor. By the time you've reached the proofreading stage, you should have already tackled all three previous types of edits.

But Jenna, this seems like a lot of editors. Are you sure I need all of them?

In theory, yes. If you're worried about hiring four different people, many editors offer packages covering more than one edit. Some seasoned writers are able to skip an editing step due to extensive practice and experience, but never impulsively assume you're one of those writers.

Now that you know what to look for, where do you find these hidden rascals? Fortunately, they're not actually hidden. Unfortunately, there are thousands of editors and "editors" to choose from, which makes the decision-making process more than a little overwhelming. Not everyone falls within the same price range, and not everyone is legitimate. How do you know if you're choosing the perfect editor for your manuscript?

Having been through this search multiple times, I've discovered some tried and true steps for selecting the ideal editor for you and your project. This can be a slow, sometimes tedious process, but I encourage you to take your time.

HOW TO CHOOSE AN EDITOR

References

There are many ways to check an editor's references. You can ask your writer friends who they've worked with and recommend; this method has never failed me. Don't have any published writer friends yet? Most of the time, authors will thank their editors in the Acknowledgment section of their books or list them on the copyright page. Find books you love with flawless prose and check those pages.

If you're still at a loss, lists of editors can be found on various websites like Reedsy, the Alliance of Independent Authors, and New York Book Editors, to name a few.

Check their website

Once you have a starting list of editors, review their websites. Look at their qualifications and credentials. Do they have certifications in editing or belong to a professional editing organization? Great. Is their website riddled with spelling errors? Not so great.

Please note, not all editors list their credentials online. This doesn't necessarily mean they're pulling the wool over your eyes, especially if they've come highly recommended by credible sources. If you're curious, ask them.

Another way to get somewhat personal referrals is to look at their testimonials page if they have one. Obviously, they're going to have glowing reviews of their services on their website, but dive deeper by searching for the books they've edited on Amazon. The Look Inside feature can be a good indicator of how well the book is edited, as well as the Amazon reviews themselves. I've found typos on page one and lengthy reviews damning the book's grammar. Editors do not get final say in the edit—writers can override their suggestions if they please—

but it's not exactly promising if these messy books are listed among their testimonials.

Specialties

Sometimes developmental editors have specialties based on genres and categories. Maybe they adore all things fantasy or they only work with young adult fiction. This kind of insight can be extra helpful if your book matches their expertise. If you're writing a high fantasy novel, then a contemporary romance editor is probably a bad choice for you.

Editors often list their specialties on their websites. If that's not available, just ask. Most editors work with a wide variety of genres but might also have some absolute no-goes—for example, children's books, nonfiction, graphic violence, or erotica.

Rates

While researching, note how much each editor charges. You'll see fees ranging widely depending on the type of edit offered; for example, developmental edits almost always cost more than copyedits, as they're working with a rougher, less-polished story. Conversely, proofreads are always very inexpensive in comparison, typically a fraction of a cent per word.

I'd love to tell you the industry average rates per editing style, but unfortunately, that's hard to nail down. The Editorial Freelancers Association (EFA) offers publicly available rates for editors to use as a guideline. However, it's quite common for editors to charge less than the available figures in order to be competitive. For example, the EFA recommends that fiction copyeditors charge $0.02 - $0.029 per word, but I often see copyeditors charging $0.01 - $0.015 per word.

Study the editors on your list and compare their rates. If some of them are offering astronomically higher rates, that's a red flag. If they're the steal of a lifetime, that's also concerning.

Sample

Most editors are willing to offer a sample edit to give you an idea of their process. This can be anywhere from three pages to three chapters and depends on the editor in question. Personally, I've usually been offered ten-page samples.

Keep in mind, editors are not required to offer sample edits. It's within their rights to say no, especially if they already have a hefty workload. But having a sample edit is a great way to determine whether this editor is a good fit for your project. It's nice to see exactly what their editing style looks like—for example, if they give lengthy explanations and assessments, or if they're straightforward and to the point. I would highly recommend at least asking for a sample, especially if you're feeling good about the editor.

For me, the sample edit usually determines who I end up hiring. If I'm interested in seeing their process, that means everything else about them has checked out. All that's left is to see their work. Some writers even put known mistakes into their samples just to see if the editor catches and corrects them. If you dig their style, fantastic. If not, onto the next.

Chemistry

Sometimes an editor ticks all the right boxes. They work within your genre and category, they have competitive rates, their website is solid, and the sample edit went great. That doesn't necessarily mean they're the person for the job. Chemistry is important when hiring anyone, and poor communication can ruin the editing process.

Pay attention to your back-and-forths. Are you getting along well? Are they punctual in their response time? Is their editing style too soft for you, or too curt? Gut instinct exists for a reason, and if this person doesn't mesh with you, keep looking. I've made the mistake of hiring an editor I didn't vibe with solely because they were highly recommended, and I ended up having a miserable experience. If anything about your interactions feels off, keep looking.

You should never choose an editor without talking to them first. Send them an email, start a dialog, and ask them questions. Make sure you're in full agreement regarding the project at hand: the estimated time frame, what this level of edit will entail, the costs involved, and how the payments will be transacted. If they make far-fetched promises, like "instant bestseller!" or "one-day turnaround!", that's not promising. No one can guarantee you sales, and no one can get a lengthy novel thoroughly edited in a matter of hours.

Make sure you feel good about the relationship and that you're both on the same page—literally and figuratively.

See? The editing process doesn't have to be so scary. Once it's over, and you have a squeaky-clean manuscript at your fingertips, we can tackle the last step of the writing process: figuring out when you're really, truly, officially done writing the book.

SUMMARY

THE PROFESSIONAL EDIT

- Types of Professional Edits:

  - Developmental edit: the big picture edits, focusing on plot, characterization, pacing, tone, and other larger elements of your story.
  - Line edit: a line-level analysis of your book, including style and readability.
  - Copyedit: focuses on the mechanics of your writing, such as grammar, spelling, and punctuation.
  - Proofread: ensures there aren't any lingering typos or formatting errors.

- How to pick an editor:

  - Ask writer friends for referrals or check trusted sources online.
  - Look at their qualifications and credentials. Do they have certifications in editing or belong to a professional editing organization? Is their website riddled with spelling errors?
  - Editors often list their specialties on their websites. If that's not available, ask them. Make sure they edit the genre you're writing.

- Compare rates. Is one editor charging much more or much less than the others? That might be a bad sign.
- Most editors will be willing to offer a sample edit if you ask for one. Having a sample edit is a great resource because you can see their work firsthand.
- Chemistry reveals itself in a variety of ways. Trust your gut and hire someone who has the editing and communication style you prefer.

CHAPTER 26
ARE WE THERE YET?

PUT A FORK IN IT, IT'S DONE

CONGRATULATIONS, you're here! The manuscript is written, edited, and waiting for you in all its glory. Does that mean it's done?

Well . . . that depends.

Sometimes—okay, a lot of the time—it's difficult to tell when you've finished your manuscript and can officially call it a book. Writers tend to obsess at this phase. Maybe we've missed something. Maybe the editor missed something. Maybe we're not real writers after all. Oh my god, should we just set this manuscript on fire and end it all?

Deep breaths and positive affirmations. It's normal to freak out right now. This is a big deal! Instead of going full pyro on your manuscript, let's examine the telltale signs your manuscript has reached its final form and is ready for publication.

You've checked off every step of the writing process

If you're like me, you probably have a list, vision board, or spreadsheet detailing every step of the writing process. If you're not like me, get on my level. I gave you this book, after all.

The writing process has roughly five billion steps. We covered all of them here, but in matter-of-fact detail and without all the drinking and crying. Crafting a story can be long and tedious. Sometimes writers are tempted to skip a step or ten, and it's reflected in their final product. If you've cut corners, readers are going to notice because your book isn't finished. But if you've been a good writer and have treated your manuscript with the care and attention it deserves, you're likely done.

You've covered every step of the professional edit

Did you only spring for a developmental editor despite your complete ineptitude at comma placement? Even worse, did you skip the professional edit entirely, opting to have your mom proofread your manuscript instead?

I included a chapter on professional editing because it's a mandatory step of the writing process. Your story is not a book unless it's edited. When you go to the department store, you expect to find a pair of jeans, not strips of denim, loose buttons, and thread. A manuscript without an edit is the same as a garment merely pinned together—unfinished.

I know you're special. I know you're talented. I know your mom used to teach second grade English. But you still need to hire an editor. If you haven't, your book isn't done.

Your editor says so

Professional editors are exactly that: professionals.

It's their job to assess the quality of your work, which means they can tell you where you're at in the publishing process. Wrangle your courage and ask them whether *they* believe your book is done.

Sometimes they'll give you a resounding yes. Other times they'll recommend a proofread. And sometimes they'll recommend another cycle of developmental changes, because holy shit, your manuscript is *rough*.

None of these answers are bad. Any information that helps you improve the quality of your story is wonderful and necessary. Trust your editor's guidance and follow suit.

You've proofread it more than once

You've hired the appropriate editors and a proofreader, yes? Fantastic. But I still recommend proofreading the novel yourself once, twice, or even five times. After all, these people are human beings, and we're all inherently flawed. They may miss a thing or two, and usually they do. I've yet to finish the editing process with a one hundred percent flawless manuscript. I always find at least a couple of lingering mistakes. Two to three typos aren't a big deal, but don't you want your book to be as clean as it can be?

Read your proofread manuscript a handful of times. If you're not so great at grammar and punctuation, enlist a few writer friends to do the same. You can also run your manuscript through ProWritingAid one more time. Consider this your last line of defense to ease your worry before publication.

You're sick of it

Readers love to ask authors if they enjoy reading their own books solely for pride or leisure. If the book was a recent release, most authors will laugh maniacally and respond with a resounding "*Hell* no."

By the time your book is published, you should have read it so many times, you're sick of it. Sure, you recognize and appreciate its quality, and you're deeply passionate about the story. But you've also memorized entire passages and can practically hear the characters prattling on in your head. Believe it or not, you can love your book and still find it annoying.

If the idea of reading your book one more time makes you want to throw up, cry, or a sad and disgusting combination of both, then congratulations, you're probably done. I've yet to meet an author come their release who wasn't beyond ready to put the book away for at least a year.

People have read it and loved it

You may be scared of rejection, an inevitable part of publishing, or plagiarism, a mostly futile fear. Regardless, you need eyes on your work —impartial readers who are willing to deliver the honest truth. At this point, you should've had many: critique partners, beta readers, sensitivity readers, and editors, to name a few.

Maybe you've been lazy. Only a couple people have read your book, but on the plus side, they loved it! Unfortunately, that doesn't do you a whole lot of good, as you need a larger sample size to truly tell if your story is at the level it needs to be.

If you haven't yet, now's the time to recruit readers to look through your manuscript and give you the hard truth. During the critique and beta reader phase, you'll likely receive a great deal of criticism. However, at this point of the process, any critiques you receive should be at a minimum. You may be dabbling in Advanced Reader Copy (ARC) territory, which is when writers send copies of their soon-to-be-published book to eager readers in return for an honest review. Are most of these ARC reviews positive, or is it a mixed bag?

Please keep in mind, not everyone will love your book. At no point in your career will you receive one hundred percent glowing praise. But if half of your ARC readers are expressing concern, giving negative criticism, or ghosting entirely, then your book probably isn't finished.

You just know

There's a lot to be said about intuition. Sometimes, beneath the worry and imposter syndrome, there's a voice deep within you saying, "Shut up and publish the book."

Instinct can be hard to decipher at times. Is it your anxiety talking, or is it your ego? From my experience, anxiety is the voice throwing out what-ifs and doomsday theories. Ego is the voice demanding you ignore all criticism, however valid, for you are the specialest specialler to ever special. Intuition, on the other hand, is something speaking softly behind all that nonsense—a voice in the back of your mind calmly stating what you already know to be true.

Does the book *feel* done? Is there something within you ready to put the keyboard down, not out of exhaustion or defeat, but out of sweet, comfortable triumph?

Again, I encourage you to make this decision after you've covered the previous steps we've gone over, but the key here is to ignore the voice in your head that's second guessing yourself. You're nervous, and that's normal. This is your book baby, and you want it to be the best it can be. But if you've done your due diligence, it's time to make the call.

The book is finished because *you* say so.

SUMMARY

ARE WE THERE YET?

- How to know if your book is done:

- You've checked off every step of the writing process.
- You've covered every step of the professional edit without skipping editors.
- Ask your editor for their opinion. Do they recommend another edit, or do they think the book is done?
- Even after the professional proofread, enlist your writer friends to read your story one more time or do another pass through ProWritingAid.
- If the thought of reading your book again makes you want to throw up or cry, then you're probably done.
- People have read your book and loved it. This sample size needs to be larger than a few people. Not everyone will love your book, but a strong majority should enjoy it.
- Sometimes you can feel that the book is complete. The book is done because you've decided it's done, but only after you've covered the previous steps. We're all nervous, and that's okay!

- Jenna is proud of you, even if she doesn't want to admit it. It doesn't bode well with her brand.

WHAT NOW?

YOU DID IT!

You've written a whole entire book.

Either that or you're like me, and you read this guide before diving into the writing process. Great minds think alike. Do people still say *twinning*? Listen, I promised to be honest, not hip.

Regardless, if you've gotten this far, you may be wondering what your next step should be. That depends on your journey. The next step may be to shut up and write the book, as I've said already. Or you've already written the book, and you may feel as though this chapter in your life has come to an end.

Hardly.

Your manuscript may be ready to go, but it isn't quite a book yet. There's still formatting, copyrighting, cover art, and a ton of marketing to do, along with every other step of publishing.

Don't let this discourage you. This moment is extremely special. You've done what millions set out to do and fail to accomplish: writing a book from start to finish. You've taken the steps necessary to make your writing process as smooth, professional, and enjoyable as possible. This is a feat. Revel in it. You deserve to feel confident and deeply proud. *I'm proud of you*, and that should count for something. I'm a hard bitch to impress.

Be sure to check out the resources at the back of this book. I've got apps and software listed that have been crucial to my writing process, and they may help you too. Still feeling insecure about the endeavor ahead? Reference this guide as much as you please. Highlight the crap out of it. That's exactly what it's here for—to act as your partner in crime through every step of the process.

Remember what I said in the last chapter: Deep breaths and positive affirmations. Hell, throw in a celebratory pizza, because you deserve it.

Now shut up and write the next book, or at the very least get this one ready for publication.

This is your time to shine.

WANT MORE?

Want more content? **Sign up for Jenna Moreci's newsletter for book release notifications, exclusive updates, special sales, and giveaways.** You'll also receive a free copy of her short story, *Great Love*, a behind-the-scenes look at her dark fantasy romance series, *The Savior's Series*.

Sign up now: https://bit.ly/jennamorecinews

ALSO BY JENNA MORECI

"Utterly unputdownable. Compulsive, addictive, and mesmerizing."

- Sacha Black, Bestselling Fantasy and Writing Craft Author

Looking for books filled with deadly tournaments, forbidden lovers, hidden magic, and much more? Check out the first two installments of Jenna Moreci's award-winning, bestselling dark fantasy romance series, ***The Savior's Series***.

ABOUT THE AUTHOR

 Jenna Moreci is a bestselling dark fantasy romance and writing craft author, as well as a YouTube sensation with hundreds of thousands of subscribers. Her first installment in The Savior's Series, *The Savior's Champion,* was voted one of the Best Books of All Time by Book Depository.

Born and raised in Silicon Valley, Jenna spends her free time snuggling up with her charming partner and their tiny dog, Buttercup.

JennaMoreci.com

youtube.com/jennamoreci

tiktok.com/@jennamoreci

patreon.com/jennamoreci

twitter.com/jennamoreci

instagram.com/jennamoreci

facebook.com/authorjennamoreci

RESOURCE GUIDE

FOR WRITING AND PLANNING:

Milanote: https://milanote.com
NovelPad: https://bit.ly/novelpad
Microsoft Word: https://www.microsoft.com/microsoft-365
Google Docs: https://www.google.com/docs/about/
Pinterest: https://www.pinterest.com

FOR EDITING AND REVISING:

ProWritingAid: https://bit.ly/jennaprowritingaid
Edit Out loud: https://bit.ly/editoutloud
Sensitivity reader Samantha Kassé: https://www.samanthakasse.com
Sensitivity reader Iona Wayland: https://ionawayland.wixsite.com/author
Reedsy: https://reedsy.com
The Alliance of Independent Authors: https://www.allianceindependentauthors.org
New York book editors: https://nybookeditors.com
The Editorial Freelancers Association: http://www.the-efa.org

FOR GENRE RESEARCH AND ANALYTICS:

K-lytics: https://bit.ly/klytics

REFERENCES

1. *The Heroine's Journey* by Gail Carriger

2. *Save the Cat!* by Blake Snyder

3. *Save the Cat! Writes a Novel* by Jessica Brody

BULK DISCOUNT?

Interested in buying 10 or more copies of SHUT UP AND WRITE THE BOOK?

Contact mail@jennamoreci.com for our discount schedule.

Please be sure to write "bulk discount" in the subject line.